TOKACHI MILLENNIUM FOREST

TOKACHI MILLENNIUM FOREST

PIONEERING A NEW WAY OF GARDENING WITH NATURE

DAN PEARSON

WITH MIDORI SHINTANI

filbert press

CONTENTS

8 FOREWORD
by Fergus Garrett

10 PREFACE

12 THE IDEA

26 THE LANDSCAPE
44 Nature worship in Japan

50 THE DESIGN

72 THE FOREST
94 Hands for the forest

100 THE EARTH GARDEN

116 THE PRODUCTIVE GARDENS
140 From earth to table

146 THE MEADOW GARDEN

166 THE MEADOW PLANTS
232 Finding your own wild

238 WORKING THE GARDENS
264 The gardenership

272 ENDNOTE
Hillside and back to nature

274 THE PLANT MIXES

278 RESOURCES

280 INDEX

FOREWORD

Fergus Garrett

Beauty and elegance are not rigidly definable. The essence of beauty is subjective and, whilst western society does not focus on elegance as an important aspect of beauty, it permeates every aspect of Japanese art and aesthetics. The Tokachi Millennium Forest epitomises this. In my eyes it is the most complex, rich and dynamic piece of design I've seen. The idealized vision, the process of transition and transformation and the extraordinarily subtle juxtaposition of east and west, make it very special.

The forest and the land surrounding are no longer downtrodden. With meaning and expression there has been reinvigoration. Stylistically the cue has been from nature and the recuperation of its values has been accomplished with the utmost empathy and understanding. The result heightens its expression and enriches the journey. The cultural traditions of the place, coupled with the voice of the landscape, the thoughtful use of negative space, interpolated with broad brushes of the ornamental, have resulted in something inimitably captivating.

The root of the success of the Millennium Forest has been through the coming together of thoughtful and like-minded souls. Firstly, a considerate and visionary owner, Mr. Hayashi, eager to nurture the forest, to return appropriated love and energy back to the land and, through this process, educate future generations. Then a deeply perceptive landscape architect, Fumiaki Takano, with the imagination and foresight to engage a western designer, Dan Pearson. Takano's move was risky but inspired, marrying east and west in the most remarkable and absolute way and key to the uniqueness of the project. Dan would undoubtedly bring a flavour of the contemporary, whilst still approaching his work with the utmost consideration. In the most respectful manner he has enhanced the spare and enriched the void. It is a lesson in the power and importance of observing. Also key has been the caring hand of a highly skilled and deeply committed head gardener, Midori Shintani, with her actions deeply rooted in the culture of her people, yet also acutely aware of the west. Midori is dedicated and totally immersed in the concept and she and Dan have developed a unique bond, a seamless and formidable partnership.

The result is spiritually and physically respectful and in tune with the earth. It is also genuinely exciting and profoundly creative – an embrace of the cultivated alongside the wild, a strengthening of the atmospheric reality and a reverence for nature, bringing out the nuances of mountain and forest, the ebb and flow of the weather and seasons, intensifying the relationship with Mother Nature.

My visits to the Millennium Forest have left lasting impressions – the power and radiant beauty of the countryside, the grace of its people, and the richness of its flora. The gardens allow you to experience the wealth and diversity of the wilderness

at arm's reach without venturing into the unknown. The intimacy of the forest, with its boardwalks and trails penetrating a world of dappled shade and woodland jewels nurtured back to life, is profoundly restorative. The mountains are brought closer and to scale by the Earth Garden which, with its undulations and mimicry, in turn forms the link to the Meadow Garden. This is Dan's masterpiece which ties everything together. Here, an intricately sinuous garden tapestry radiates out from a central space. On closer inspection Dan's bold brushstrokes reveal complex communities, dynamic and multi-layered, rich with life, overflowing with texture. Natives and exotics share the same ground and form a link to the world beyond. There is a sophistication here, befitting the culture and people it serves. With the lightest of touches he has brought the wider landscape in, and taken the garden out, transitioning one into the other. This is the work of a highly knowledgeable and gifted plantsman and gardener.

Dan is the most sensitive and deeply connected designer I know. He has an innate ability to grasp the multifarious forces defining the sense of place. This, coupled with an acutely observant eye, results in someone extraordinarily in tune with the surrounding natural aesthetic. Poetic in his way with plants, his brilliant, creative mind rides abreast a deep and profound respect for the language of the land. His sympathetic, considerate, highly original and thought-provoking schemes speak of a deep inner emotional life.

Dan is also an instinctive ecologist – someone who understands habitats and plant communities – an artist united with the wilder world. And here there is a clear synergy with our work at Great Dixter, where life in and around the garden involves not only people and communities, plants and creativity, but also an inbuilt curiosity and respect for the microcosm of life with which we share our space. The biodiversity-rich habitats in both gardens are closely connected with the wild land surrounding them. Flowing, interconnecting environments lightly touched by human hand.

The story is beautifully articulated in Dan and Midori's words and emotionally conveyed in exceptional photos, making this a most stimulating and intelligent book.

Page 2: Aesculus turbinata, the Japanese chestnut, is native to Hokkaido and Honshu.

Page 4: A dew-spangled dragonfly on a seedhead of *Lysimachia clethroides* in the Meadow Garden.

Pages 6-7: Dawn breaks over the Hidaka Mountains in early spring.

Above: Midori Shintani, Fergus Garrett and Dan Pearson in the Meadow Garden in 2012.

PREFACE

This is a story about a singular vision which started nearly 30 years ago, when Mitsushige Hayashi set out to make his newspaper business carbon neutral. In many ways he was ahead of his time and now, with our very real fears about the environment being played out in front of us, his ambition for the Millennium Forest to be "a garden for a thousand years", could not be more fitting.

It has been a remarkable opportunity to be part of this vision and to help to make a place that re-engages people with nature and their environment. It is a vision that asks us to contemplate a thousand years of custodianship; a timeframe that is beyond us but is nevertheless thought-provoking and starts to engage us from the moment we hear about it.

The ambition to protect this place, and to encourage people who visit the forest to come to love it, is at the heart of the idea. It is an idea that has positive influence, that inspires us to do something and feel empowered by our engagement.

The Millennium Forest is a team effort. The Hayashi family are the enablers and the team that look after the forest do so with commitment. I see this most directly through my working relationship and now friendship with Head Gardener Midori Shintani and Assistant Head Gardener Shintaro Sasagawa, who understand the gardens and the way the forest works so thoroughly. It is their life and their way of being and the land sings quietly for their devotion. The moment you place your foot on the soil of the woodland path is a potent one and I believe wholeheartedly that this remarkable place has a reach that will travel far beyond these pages.

Miscanthus sinensis 'Zebrinus' in the Meadow Garden.

THE IDEA

My Introduction to the Project

In 1997, I made a television series with Channel 4 which explored the art of garden-making beyond British shores. We travelled to Japan to look at a culture that reached back centuries and drew upon a strong tradition of its own making and then went on to North America, where the influences were altogether different for being more recent and outward looking.

I had long been fascinated by the Japanese approach to gardens – the order, the reverence for nature and the close observation of it. It was a world that seemed altogether more sophisticated than the West in its perspective on the subject and, though I admit to trepidation about the associated austerity, my heart was already open.

We made two trips to Japan for filming, the first in the autumn to reconnoitre the places and the people who would help us unravel the stories and the second in the month of April to film during *hanami*, the cherry blossom season. These first encounters proved to be transformative. To discover that there was such a developed language of observing and revealing nuances felt like a homecoming. I found it in the seasonality of the food that we ate, such as the quiet theatre of an autumnal bento box with ginkgo fruit and a sprig of pine needles to mark the moment, in a May kimono printed with iris, in the *furin* (wind chimes) put up in the summer to call the coolness by giving the breeze form in sound, and in the beautiful wrapping of the most mundane purchases. It was a sensual world where ways of seeing were ritualized to make you appreciate your environment more deeply. A reverence for detail and the essence of things was everywhere present in the day to day.

I began my essential reading. *In Praise of Shadows* by Junichiro Tanizaki explores the importance of taking time to pay attention to the smallest things and the culture of finding the beauty in the dark, in-between places, such as the power of lacquer ware for its tactile, reflective and luminous qualities in the cool of a dark interior. He even laments the passing of the dimly lit toilet in favour of brightly lit and sanitized modernity, regarding the moments of lost contemplation during the time passed in this little room as being particular and valuable.

I learned too about the importance of wabi and sabi, the traditional Japanese aesthetic sense of finding beauty in imperfection and accepting transience, the natural cycle of growth, decay and death. It was a remarkable thing to be shown a way of seeing that seemed to connect very deeply with the ephemeral world I saw through observing gardens and nature. To be allowed to appreciate the simple, the slow and the uncluttered and a reverence for authenticity was quite simply to receive the gift of time.

A traditional Japanese garden in Kyoto seen through a bamboo screen.

Close observation was a process that I was intuitively using myself, but had no vocabulary for. However, I knew that I had stumbled upon a place and a philosophy that I wanted to explore more deeply. It was to be the start of a long and fascinating journey. A perfect example of the revelation was an evening spent at a *sakura* (cherry tree) nursery just outside Kyoto. A king Yoshino cherry (*Prunus × yedoensis*), tended to perfection over several generations, had been illuminated from beneath by flaming braziers. It was the gloaming hour and the point at which the first breaking buds announced the shift from winter to spring. We stood in awe and quiet celebration as time slowed in the flickering tree branches.

Another moment was distilled at Saihoji Temple where, before you are allowed into the revered moss garden, you must sit with the monks and chant with them or trace over the written chant with brush and ink on paper. This time of slowing, meditation and reflection calms the mind and body and so allows the detail in the garden to come into a new focus. The mossy understorey is soon revealed to be not just one green, but multiple greens of many different textures. In an area of the garden you are drawn to look at stones arranged to mimic a dry river bed, the energy of their placement suggesting the movement of water, which in your mind's eye you can see racing and turbulent. Only carp rising to break the water of the still ponds interrupt a quiet that you are lulled into and, for a moment, there are no radios or traffic beyond the boundaries. It is a sensual garden of feelings which suspends you in a heightened awareness far more extensive than its physical reach. Over time I have grown to deeply appreciate the art of nature worship in Japan, for its appearance in daily life and in the places where you are taken to a whole different level of communing with the natural world.

Three years after my first visit in 1997, Fumiaki Takano invited me to speak at a landscape conference in Sapporo on the island of Hokkaido. One of the people we had met and interviewed during the filming, Takano was a new breed of Japanese landscape architect and looked out into the world rather than back to tradition for his inspiration. We had enjoyed each other's company during filming, he being interested in my naturalistic approach to the subject and me in his innovative approach to collaboration and the making of places for people.

After the lectures, he invited me back east and so we travelled from Sapporo to the region of Tokachi, where we spent the next three days exploring. His practice was based in an old schoolhouse in the town of Otofuke and it became clear during the course of the time we spent together that there was a project in the offing. Each day presented a more intimate reveal of what it might be. On the first day I met his team and we made soba noodles together in the schoolhouse. On the second day, the group became smaller and we went up into the mountains to visit a frozen lake where they had created a temporary settlement of ice buildings and enclosures to celebrate winter. The next day we set out as a group of five to explore the woods on skis and later the same day ascended in a hot air balloon to see the landscape from above.

1. The bamboo grove at Arashiyama, Kyoto 2. Saihoji temple moss garden 3. Cherry blossom at hanami time 4. A house covered in bonsai in Kyoto

1

2

3

4

Looking down from
Millennium Hill onto the
agricultural clearances that
run away into the flatlands
that lie on the edge of
the Millennium Forest. The
Earth Garden can be
seen to the left.

1

2

3

4

At the end of the last day Takano and his business partner, Kanekiyo, took me up into the mountains in a jeep. It was dark by the time we pulled off the road and headed into the trees. After a short walk along a snowy ridge we could hear the sound of rushing water, which we followed by dipping down into a small ravine. Just below us, steaming in the reflected half-light from the snow, was a hot spring (*onsen*), makeshift in construction but clearly the object of our walk. It was just large enough for the three of us and we stripped and climbed quickly into hot water, our knees touching and our heads from the chin up in the freezing air. It was -25°C (-13°F) and my hair froze from the steam that came off the water and rapidly condensed.

Takano's wife had sent us on our excursion with three bags, each of which contained a small towel and a can of Sapporo beer. We sat there soaking as Takano explained the nature of the project, the passion of a local newspaper magnate for it and the masterplan they had devised together to make an ecological park that would be sustainable for a thousand years. Finally, as the moon swung around the mountain and lit the ravine we were nestled into, the offer of a collaboration came. Would I work with them to help make it happen?

Mr Hayashi and the big idea

Tokachi Millennium Forest is the brainchild of the entrepreneur Mitsushige Hayashi, who acquired the land with a view to offsetting the carbon footprint of his national newspaper business, Tokachi Mainichi. The Hayashi family settled in Hokkaido in 1897 and Mr Hayashi has a deep attachment to the land and to trying to protect it for future generations. By the year 2000, the area he purchased amounted to 400 hectares (988 acres). The flat agricultural land at the base of the mountain rolls steeply up into foothills where bears live in the forests and nature is still king.

When I first met Mr Hayashi and we walked the site it was clear that the land resonated for him on a spiritual level. He explained to me that there was power in the erratics that had been moved from the mountain by ancient glaciers and now littered the forest. He spoke in animistic terms, explaining how all the components of this place have spiritual power, and how he desired to protect the spirit of the land. Although Mr Hayashi told me that research showed that the aboriginal people of Hokkaido, the Ainu, had never lived here, he talked of their importance as the original people who had made the island their home and worked its rivers and woodland long before it was settled by the Japanese. He had chosen this particular area because he believed that it had a special place at the base of the mountains with its own energy and gravity.

Not long after he acquired the original plot of land in 1990, Mr Hayashi started forest management with the Shimizu Forestry Association. Then, in 1996, he enlisted Takano Landscape Planning (TLP) to produce a masterplan to help make the land viable and create a public park. The project was intended to help redress the balance between man and the natural environment and to allow people the opportunity to be part of

1. Assessing the Tokachi landscape by balloon in January 2003 2. Fumiaki Takano (in red) and his team at Takano Landscape Planning at their Hokkaido office 3. One of the many erratics left on the site in the last ice age 4. The first invaders after wholesale logging are pioneer species such as native birch, *Betula platyphylla* (shirakanba) and sasa bamboo, *Sasa nipponica*, (kumazasa)

nature and observe it at close quarters. Mr Hayashi's big idea was a vision of a park with sustainability for a thousand years. This lateral thinking set out not only to make the newspaper business carbon neutral (which, as of 2019, it has become by more than 120%), but also to preserve this area of the island and prevent further loss of habitat to development and agriculture. The reality of the thousand-year vision is, of course, something that we have little control over in terms of climate change and extreme weather events, for instance, but for the wider ambition of a reconnection with nature to be viable Mr Hayashi believes that education is key. Encouraging its users to take ownership of the concept of longevity is the best way to ensure the land's future, one generation investing and handing on responsibility to the next.

In a country that sees the greater part of the population urbanized and far removed from landscape and nature, the idea of getting people engaged with the environment is a powerful one. The volcanic terrain here is elemental, the skies are big and the weather whistles over the Hidaka mountain range that backdrops the site. Spring snowmelt rushes through the forests in clear, fast-moving streams and the storms that have passed through in the time that I have been involved have been humbling. Bridges were swept away during the typhoon of 2016 and stone from the mountain washed down in the torrents that weave through the site. Remarkably, the floods parted around the gardens, but our efforts to do the best for the land immediately felt small and irrelevant. Here, when nature demonstrates it is bigger, you are put very firmly in your place. That said, it is the scale of things that makes this place remarkable.

When Takano asked for my involvement, it was to pick up on the initial thinking and to help provide another layer to ground the visitor. I identified early on that any changes we planned to make had to be in tune with the greater order of the place. They would also need to be in scale – bold enough not to feel tentative, but very much in context so that the magnitude of the place was complemented by intimacy. The passage into being part of the landscape would play upon a process of discovery. An important part of this approach would look to the ritual of close observation, a gentle reveal prompted by an intuitive meeting with nature. A path that passes a rock to allow the visitor the opportunity of observing the way the light falls upon it; the gravity of a stone providing a spot to rest or a signal to the next place on the trail; a safe crossing over rapidly moving water that provides immediate delight, but also makes the visitor aware of its source ahead, high up in the mountain.

The work we have done to help make people feel comfortable in the landscape aims to slowly draw them out and gently acclimatize them after the comfort of urban living. Paths that lead the way from place to place become progressively more rugged and as the visitor becomes accustomed to there being mud underfoot, the way is already made less fearful. Through providing a more intimate connection to the environment we hoped to kindle in visitors an enduring relationship with this place, one that would be passed from generation to generation and so ensure the park's future.

Opposite: The stepping stone crossing to the Forest Garden was made after the 2016 typhoon swept away the previous bridge.

Overleaf: The garden team in the Earth Garden looking towards Millennium Hill where a horseback tour group ventures into the wider landscape.

THE LANDSCAPE

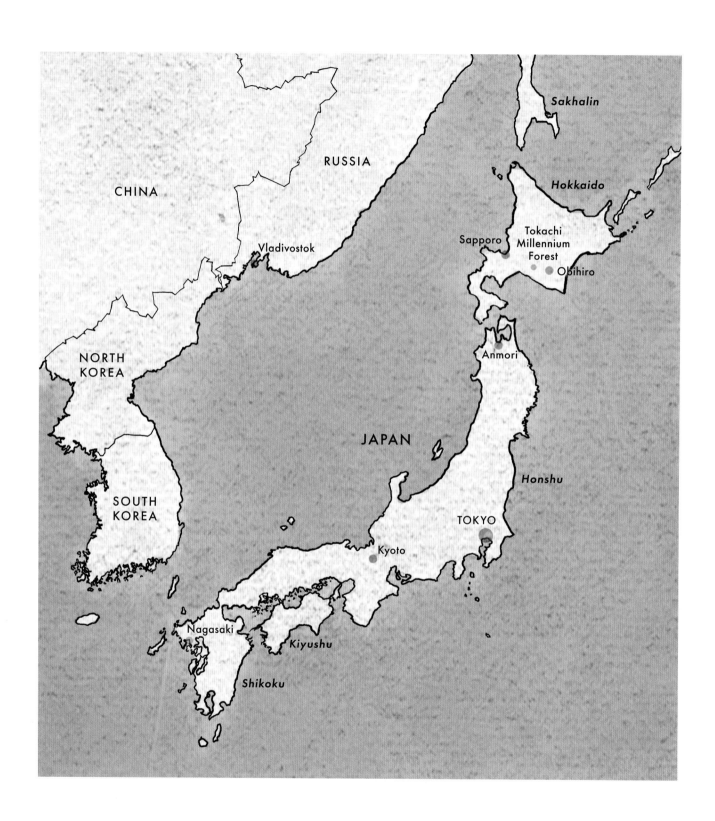

Context

The northernmost island of the Japanese archipelago and just two hours' flight north of Tokyo, Hokkaido is almost equivalent in size to Ireland. Winter is the dominant season and it arrives early, the autumn colouring in September, the landscape whited-out and chilled to -25°C (-13°F) at its coldest. Snow is often still on the ground at the end of April, so the growing season is compressed and accelerates quickly. This is a lush landscape in the summer months, with plenty of moisture, hot sun and night-time temperatures that are reliably cool and ideal for a productive season of agriculture.

Hokkaido was once connected to Russia via a land bridge when sea levels were lower, but it was never joined by bridge to the main island of Honshu. Today, the Seikan Tunnel passes beneath the Tsugaru Strait and connects the Aomori prefecture on Honshu island with Hokkaido. With a length of 23km (14 miles) at 140m (459ft) below the seabed, this is the world's deepest and longest railway tunnel. If you travel to Hokkaido by plane from Tokyo, the journey is always marked by stepping into a cooler climate, somewhere detached from the age-old culture of Honshu.

With its small population and wide open spaces, it comes as no surprise to find that the island has only been widely colonized since the late 1800s. Although initial attempts at Japanese occupation of the island began in the 15th century, until that time the land was primarily occupied by the Ainu, an indigenous population of hunter-gatherers. The Ainu worked the rivers during the summer months, plant-gathering and salmon fishing, while from late autumn to early summer, when vegetation had withered but game was plentiful in the fields and the mountains, they hunted. Their animist religion was based on a reverence for natural phenomena, geological features, the elements, flora and fauna.

Trading in the 1800s saw the Ainu become increasingly dependent upon the main island of Honshu, and in 1899 the Japanese passed an act designating the Ainu as 'former aborigines' and granting them automatic Japanese citizenship, which effectively denied them the status of an indigenous group; it was only in April 2019, following decades of campaigning, that the Japanese government finally passed legislation officially recognizing the Ainu as an indigenous people. By the early 1900s the Japanese were moving to Hokkaido for its natural resources. Roads and bridges were built to extract oak lumber from the forests and the rich alluvial valleys were cleared and developed for agriculture with the use of heavy horses. The dairy industry progressed in Hokkaido when, in 1876, William Smith Clark, an American professor of agriculture, was invited to share his newest thinking and asked to establish the Sapporo

The Tokachi Millennium Forest is located on Hokkaido, the most northern of the main islands in the Japanese archipelago.

Agricultural College, which is now Hokkaido University. Out of these rough, pioneering times with stories that tell of the first wild settlers, a new and forward-thinking culture was born on the island.

The land at Tokachi Millennium Forest bears witness to this development. The flatlands running from the sea to the foot of the Hidaka Mountains have been deforested and drained for arable use or pasture on rotation. The lower parts of the site sit on the edge of these, with the greater part of the land encompassing the forested foothills before the mountains take over. The forests have been logged more than once, the mature wood replaced by second-growth oak and pioneer birch where it has not been replanted with larch. This is grown at scale where access is possible and harvested for paper pulp. It is only where the slopes become inaccessible that the native forest has remained untouched.

Driving the forty-minute journey west from the town of Obihiro, you head towards the mountains that form the distant horizon. The road takes you from the town through an open hinterland of industrial warehouses and then out into agriculture. You cross more than one braided river, where the winter snowmelt can be seen in annual scars that have recently torn at willowy banks and gouged deeply into grey rocky shingle. The road soon becomes smaller and zigzags along the drainage ditches that form the boundaries of the grids of industrial-sized fields. In the summer, the linear ditches are lush with vegetation that would claim open ground, given half a chance. Giant knotweeds (*Fallopia sachalinensis*) arch their limbs and bear's angelica (*Angelica ursina*) bolt upwards to 3m (10ft) with umbels the size of dinner plates towering above your car. The ploughed ground immediately alongside is deep, coal black and highly productive with row upon row of corn, buckwheat, soy and potatoes.

The inhabitants of the farmsteads and smallholdings beat back the native vegetation and throw down brightly coloured annuals on their driveways to offset the power of the environment. Lilac trees might cling close to a barn where concession is made to aesthetics, but the buildings you see are workmanlike and utilitarian, bleak in winter. The snow-covered roads are then marked with flags to prevent you straying and the buildings are kept neat and tidy so that it is easy to work to clear the snow. There is little romance in the wintry farmland, for the managed ground is a landscape of necessities, but the forests and the mountains take on a magical, otherwordly quality.

The Hidaka mountains form a jagged horizon that backdrops the flatlands and the mood changes as they rise up to dominate the skyline. It is only when they feel reachable and you can see the scale in the texture of their flanks that a band of trees rises steeply out of the agricultural land and comes between you and the view. When this happens you pull off the road into a little car park that sits among trees, marking the spot that arrests the reach of agriculture to the mountainside beyond.

Opposite, above: The foothills with *Miscanthus sinensis* heralding autumn. *Below:* A typical scene from the Tokachi area with the agricultural plains running to the base of the Hidaka Mountains.

Overleaf: The Millennium Forest sits at the base of the mountains where forests on the lower ground were felled and replanted with larch for paper pulp. Second generation forest can be seen in the foreground, reclaiming its territory once the larch is removed.

Geography

The Hidaka mountains provide the setting for the Tokachi Millennium Forest. Snow sits high on their peaks for the greater part of the year to sharpen their outline. It is already there in September to remind you of the impending winter and is slow to retreat from the summits well into the growing season. Come summer, they are often shrouded in cloud, which hangs heavy in the woods that darken their slopes. Their volume comes and goes according to the moisture in the air, but when the sky is low and they rise into the cloud, you can still feel their weight and influence. The woods that clothe the flanks fall gently away to meet the flat, open ground that over the last century has been cleared to meet the foothills.

Energetic streams, charged with snowmelt, make their way from the mountain slopes and lace the woods that extend onto the flatter ground at the Millennium Forest. Here the watercourses reveal the undulations that, from a distance, the trees disguise. The alluvial soil, blackened by silt and leaf mould, is cut where the race of a stream reveals a pale bed of time-worn boulders. Each layer has time marked clearly and where the land has not been disturbed by man it feels aged and elemental. The streams are diverted by erratics which made their way down the valleys in previous ages. In places these rounded boulders stand hunched and proud above ground. Lichens, mosses and creeping hydrangeas hug their contours. Mr Hayashi speaks profoundly about the power of the stones, which he believes resonate with mountain energy. Their presence, which is often enormous, is something you naturally gravitate towards and feel humbled by. They make immediately understandable the Ainu belief that all forms of life and the inanimate objects in the landscape too have spiritual power.

The woods are the natural state of things here. In winter the landscape is stripped bare, for there are very few evergreens which live above the snow. The streams are hushed, capped first by ice and then the unification of snow. Then the mountains are closer and visible through the trees, the undulations in the forest revealed again beneath a neutral blanket. In summer these same woods are entirely different, the canopy closed over, a lush forest floor shadowed and humid with growth, the transparency of winter gone and the mountains held back from view.

The trees protect the ground from the rigour of the elements, which from time to time assert their power. The typhoon of late summer 2016 saw the streams which braid the woodland fully charged. Several bridges in the forest were swept away, never to be seen again, and whole new landscapes opened up as the water brought down rock and spoil from the mountain and carved new ways through the woodland. The experience was humbling and, for a time, the aspiration of a thousand years of sustainability felt very much in question. What was remarkable, however, was the counterbalance provided by the rate of growth in the following seasons, which saw the scars healed within a year.

The water which discharges from the mountains is a significant presence here, and where it doesn't appear above ground it is moving constantly below and through the site on its way to the flatlands. Despite the magnitude of the elements in the park,

Opposite: In the depths of winter the water from the mountains runs under the snow. As winter begins to lose its grip the streams reveal the change in the season.

Overleaf: The ground on the fringes of the cultivated areas is maintained for biodiversity, with rough meadows and open glades that maintain views to Millennium Hill. The same view in winter is seen on the pages that follow.

there are gentle places in the woods where a balance has been struck for a time. Rivulets that have not found their way to join a stream seep through the hollows to create woodland bogs. Skunk cabbages and marsh marigolds trace these lines to reveal what is happening and watery pools reflect the canopy of oak and magnolia.

Where the woods on the lower slopes give way to the open ground associated with clearance, the environment is one of vigorous grassland and pioneer perennials. During the brief window of high summer, the heat in the sun can be intense out in the open. As you step into the light of a bright day, you leave the scream of the cicadas behind you, for the forest interior is their domain. In the sun, and in a climate where rainfall is never far away, you can feel the charge in growth and the rush to complete a life cycle, for it will not be long before the snow appears again on the mountain.

Climate

As the cold weather comes in at the end of the autumn, the chill from Russia is marked in a driving horizontal sleet that pushes down from the mountains and skids over the contours of the Earth Garden. The winter dictates everything on the island during its half-year tenancy and during this time the landscape is beautifully black and white. Sharpened by the contrast of dark trunks and bright light reflected from snow, the outlines of trees are thrown starkly in shadow. As you attune your eyes to a grey overcast day in winter, the nuances of the apparent monochrome are revealed, with birch trunks creamy against the snow, browns and greys in the darker tree trunks and intense colour in lichens.

Visit the Sapporo region to the west and you notice that the snow is wetter and deeper. A thriving ski culture exists on this part of the island. Further east, the Tokachi region is known for the severity of its winters and the snow here is fine and powdery, rarely more than 60cm (24in) deep. Anything that stands proud of the snow has to be hardy enough to withstand average freezing temperatures of -15°C (5°F), which on some occasions dips to -25°C (-13°F). Most plants, therefore, are winter deciduous and the evergreen bamboo *Sasa nipponica* only survives because it bends under the weight of snow and remains covered. Hibernating bears make their dens under the shelter of the sasa, so you have to be careful where you tread if you stray from the paths in the woods.

The snow is the very reason why it has been possible to garden at the Millennium Forest. In a good year it arrives before the freeze gets into the ground too deeply and throws down a protective eiderdown for the perennial layer of vegetation. This allows us to grow a whole range of plants that are adapted to similar climates or are hardy enough to cope with dormancy under its protection. That said, it does appear that the climate is changing. Over the decade since the Meadow Garden was first planted, Midori has observed that the arrival of the snow is becoming less reliable, though we have yet to see significant damage where the freeze comes before the snow.

After almost half the year under snow, the garden is 'woken' in March by the gardeners casting powdered charcoal to warm the snow, before finally shovelling the garden free in the early spring. With warmth and access to light, the growing season rears into life fast and furiously at the end of April. Ground that is charged with water from the winter and reliable rainfall throughout the growing season has no need of irrigation. In the short window of summer, there is heat in the sun and plants grow quickly and reliably where they are suited.

Though the growing season is short, summer makes for good cultivation and the cool nights on Hokkaido are pivotal to both agriculture and horticulture on the island. While the night-time warmth and associated humidity on Honshu provide perfect growing conditions for fungal attacks that limit the range of hardy perennials it is possible to grow, mildews and moulds are less of a problem in the cooler temperatures of Hokkaido. Though shrubby material that pushes above the snow is limited by the conditions, the range of perennial material is opened up by the winter protection and cool summer nights.

The condensed nature of the summer makes for an applied and strategic approach to gardening. It is not uncommon to see a late frost in June, or for there to be a touch of autumn already in the garden in August, so the weeks in between demand focus. Flowering seasons of genera that span several months in the more temperate climate of the UK come together in unexpected associations and the garden changes visibly from day to day. The gardeners have to act fast when the garden is in full flush, but the winter remains the dominant season. Its sudden and complete arrival dictates that everything has to be cut back and put to bed before winter, for there is not the luxury of doing so in the rush of spring.

Opposite: Caltha palustris var. barthei is one of the first plants to emerge after snowmelt.

Overleaf: The native woodland claims the slopes where ground is too steep for logging. The Millennium Forest reaches up into this high ground, but it remains inaccessible to the public.

Midori Shintani

Nature worship in Japan

I was born and raised in the countryside, surrounded by the sea of Wakasa Bay and the mountains of the Fukui prefecture in Honshu, Japan. My childhood memory is filled with the landscape of rugged coastline, islands and fishing boats, bamboo forests behind temples, rivers flowing through the town, vast rice fields, animals and the people who lived there.

Everywhere, on the way home from school or in the field for holiday adventures, plants were always by my side. I spent a lot of time with them to make grass whistles, leaf masks and rough bouquets in the field. Once I was brimming with curiosity, they invited me to a world that I had never seen before. Attracted to the sparkling spikes of Japanese silver grass (*Miscanthus sinensis*), I got closer and was overwhelmed by their vigorous presence. I found them scary and fascinating at the same time and this fear and admiration for plants made me feel sure that I was living with them.

The Japanese archipelago stretches 3000km (1860 miles) from north to south, the mountain ranges running through it like a backbone. Nearly 70 per cent of the country is covered by forests. Due to its complex topography from the coast to the high mountains, as well as its diverse range of climates, Japan is a country rich in biodiversity. Since ancient times, the Japanese people established a lifestyle in this wild nature.

Our ancestors derived various resources for living by hunting and gathering from the forests. Since the introduction of agriculture, they had necessarily cut their way into the densely forested mountains and cultivated agricultural sites and spaces for living. The lower mountain areas behind the villages that they established were rich in natural resources.

Midori Shintani with the giant native umbellifer, *Angelica ursina* (ezonyu).

Above: Native miscanthus meadows are
a feature of the Honshu landscape.
Below: Rice paddy fields overlooking Wakasa Bay
in Midori's homeland of Fukui.

People lived with the blessings of nature and, sometimes in the face of natural disasters, cultivated an animistic spirit of awe and reverence. The ancient Japanese believed that the eight million Divine called *kami* dwell in every element of nature such as stone, tree, grass, mountain and animal, as well as water and wind. Our ancestors invited *kami* from primitive nature to the forests of the high mountains and set a shrine in each village, which was believed to protect people. The higher mountain area was left untouched as a sacred forest, and our ancestors restricted use of the forest areas to those immediately behind the villages. They carefully coppiced trees to harvest firewood and the cutting area was left to regenerate until the next harvest in 20 years. The water sources from the mountains supported agriculture, fallen leaves were gathered to use as fertilizer in the rice fields and people also collected various foods, housing materials and medicines from the forests, but they never destroyed the vegetation.

The areas that our ancestors efficiently utilized developed into secondary forests where living things harmoniously coexist. This particular zone between conserved mountainous areas and villages is called *satoyama*. *Satoyama* has been extended for thousands of years by small-scale agricultural and forestry use throughout the Japanese archipelago, except for Hokkaido.

It is inevitable that the natural environment will be affected in the course of human life. The existence of a shrine protecting a small village still tells us that the people living there have respected nature in gratitude and awe, and through disciplined human activities. In these and many other ways, Japanese people have learned to live in harmony with nature.

The Japanese way of life and nature changed drastically during the period of high economic growth which began with the post-war reconstruction in the 20th century. With the spread of electricity, gas, and water and sewage services, railways and expressways were constructed as transportation networks connecting big cities. As fossil fuels replaced firewood and charcoal, many of the *satoyama* forests were abandoned. Expanded afforestation of conifers such as Japanese cedar and Japanese cypress, which were useful for supplying the increasing demand for construction due to the rapidly growing economy, was promoted as the national policy. The city parks, devastated during the war, were rebuilt in accordance with the large-scale development of residential areas such as housing complexes in the 1950s and 1960s.

Rapid urbanization and industrialization led to environmental destruction and social problems such as industrial waste and pollution caused by mass production, and that reached its most serious phase in the late 1960s and early 1970s. Later, I learned about the problems of pollution from my environmental education in elementary school. It was unbelievable for me who was chasing a tadpole in a rice paddy field, but it certainly happened that large amounts of pollutants were emitted by massive industrial manufacturing, and pollution-related diseases occurred in several places in Japan.

In the mid-1970s, a long-term plan for urban greening projects was formulated by the national and prefectural governments. In the 1980s and 1990s, when it became widely known that *satoyama* was endangered, many people hoped to sustain this irreplaceable Japanese landscape. Restoration and conservation activities of *satoyama* developed into citizen activities that were contributed to not only by national organizations, but also by many local volunteer groups and non-profit organizations. The missions of corporate environmental activities were further enhanced, and the carbon offset project of the Tokachi Mainichi Newspaper Company was born at this time. This later became the Tokachi Millennium Forest.

After this period of confusion in the 20th century, we took a step toward the 21st century. The purpose of Tokachi Millennium Forest is to create a movement to build a harmonious relationship between nature and mankind for the future. Japanese nature worship is to live with sincere devotion to nature. This spirit, inherited from our ancestors, is surely alive in our forest. Our mission is to follow tradition and yet to develop it into something modern. I believe that the garden shows us its essence and connects us to the greater nature beyond.

Above: A typical *satoyama*
landscape. *Below:* Rice ricks drying in a
traditional agricultural landscape.

THE DESIGN

Understanding the place

The Tokachi Millennium Forest is a project that engages with scale. The mountains and the forest, the water that rushes through it and the dramatic transition between summer and winter provide the route into understanding the area and its order. In the greater scheme of things our role as custodians is fleeting, but by applying our energies carefully and in an informed manner, we can choose to have a positive and significant influence. This is what the masterplan set out to do, but for the big idea that the park be sustainable for a thousand years, it was imperative first to find a way to be part of the place.

By observing the land that was colonized just under 150 years ago, we could see how quickly a landscape is vulnerable to change. 'Progress' has stripped the landscape back from the dynamic habitats of forests and waterways to be replaced by fields that provide one or two crops a year at most and lie dormant in winter, waiting for the plough. The accessible forests, which were already stripped of good lumber in the first part of the last century, have in many cases been planted with larch for paper pulp. Sasa, the low-growing native bamboo, has seized the window opened with the increased light levels of felling and swept the forest floor in a resultant monoculture.

Just a handful of generations ago, the Ainu lived in harmony with the natural order of things. The land provided for the people who lived here within the ecosystem – a relationship that today would simply not be viable but, in terms of inspiration, one that can teach us how to tread more lightly and show us how people lived and worked in context with the landscape. On Honshu, the old ways of living more intimately with the land are borne out in the culture of *satoyama*. This word describes the physical area of land between pasture and forest inhabited by man as well as the ethos of living harmoniously within the landscape. It addresses a better balance, one that creates a respectful meeting place between man and the environment. The principle of a more thoughtful integration was key to the approach of the masterplan.

The site masterplan

Mr Hayashi was very aware of the toll that had been taken on the Hokkaido landscape when he bought the property. One of the first images I was shown was an aerial photograph of the site as it was in 2000, when it totalled about 400 hectares (988 acres). It showed the stark reach of agriculture, fields drained and parcelled in a formal grid that swept to the base of the mountains. This satellite image also showed us the impact

Once the oak had been extracted for timber the foothills were replanted with commercial larch. The disturbance allowed pioneering sasa to claim the forest floor and diminish floral diversity.

on the forest, with larch plantations fingering up the slopes and woods that were clearly no longer primary growth.

The site was attractive because it sat on the edge of things. Although the ordered agricultural landscape reached into its lower section and forestry had already had its impact on the slopes that were accessible, there was enough that was still elemental: mountains to provide scale and drama, streams for articulation and energy and much second-growth forest already regenerated with young oak trees. There were hinterlands of rough grassland, which had formerly been pasture and were now already frayed at the edges with pioneer woodland, and the promise of extending the site further into the mountains by acquiring more land. It was a place of stark beauty which offered a clearly defined contrast to the agricultural flatlands that reached back to the city.

Mr Hayashi's ambition was to protect this place for future generations, but in order to do that he needed to make it viable and for the project to have its own momentum. The landscape architecture practice Takano Landscape Planning was commissioned in 1996 to create a masterplan and help realize the site's potential as an ecological park. The ambition that it be sustainable for a thousand years was established. It was a big idea in terms of our human continuity, and it demanded a new way of thinking about time and our commitment to the environment as custodians.

While the masterplan was evolving, experimentation began to determine how best to regenerate the areas that had been put down to larch plantation. Some of the larch was removed in entirety from a series of slopes with different aspects to test how the forest regenerated naturally. Nearby, lighter intervention felled the larch in strips to retain local microclimates and protection for animals and regenerating native plant species. The latter approach to re-wilding yielded the best regrowth of the indigenous forest due to the protection provided by the thinned plantations.

In limited areas closer to the buildings the Millennium Forest team had also started to control the sasa, the invasive bamboo that had invaded the open ground, to seize a window of opportunity after initial logging. To redress the balance and to allow the original diversity of species their opportunity to recolonize, the sasa had been strimmed to the ground on an annual basis in the autumn. The results had been remarkable, the sasa weakened enough for the residual seedbank in the leaf-mould to rejuvenate the perennial woodland flora.

By the time I arrived on site in 2000, the process of making the site accessible had begun. A car park was already in place, along with a repurposed barn serving as a ticket office and information centre. The Entrance Forest had been thinned to allow enough light to penetrate to the floor and the sasa had been reduced to make way for the residual seedbank of woodland understorey, which in just five years had shown remarkable powers of recovery. A series of walkways led through the gentle incline of the woodland, switching to and fro against the flow of the streams that coursed from the mountains. A purpose-built restaurant on the edge of the woodland looked out over 5 hectares (12 acres) of flat pasture towards the mountains. To the left, on the edge of the site,

Opposite, above: Rigorous annual strimming of the sasa was required to allow the native flora to re-establish. *Below:* This aerial photograph of 2000, with the park boundary marked in white, illustrates the impact of agriculture upon the natural vegetation.

Overleaf: The borrowed view of the Hidaka Mountains is ever present at the edge of the forest.

a goat farm occupied a series of barns built on the edge of a similar area of pasture. The farm, which predated Mr Hayashi's arrival at the site, was small in scale but already producing award-winning cheese.

Beyond the flat pasture, trails had been cut into the woods for pedestrian access and for exploring on horseback. A single-track road laid to a foothill at the base of the mountain extended the reach of possible access. From Millennium Hill, looking back to the lowland of the entrance forest and plains, I could grasp the scale of things and understand that the site was not an intimate place. The flat paddocks of agricultural land cut a straight line unceremoniously alongside the Entrance Forest, dividing the mountains from the arrival experience. Towards Obihiro, I could see agriculture rolling off into the distance. The mountains that formed our backdrop marked a dramatic contrast and were not somewhere that felt friendly. It was difficult to get a sense of scale, and this was disquietening. The grounds felt inhospitable and not somewhere one might want to explore.

As a means of drawing visitors out into the landscape in the early days, an art trail featuring the work of Didier Courbot, Osamu Asano and Yoko Ono among others was constructed. An education programme set up with local schools to encourage good knowledge of the plants and wildlife was also in place, but the visitor experience was rough and ready and it was clear that another layer to the masterplan was needed to encourage people to stay and explore. The visitors, it seemed, were overwhelmed by the very things that made the place remarkable; the scale and the force of nature were proving to be inhibiting. On first impressions it seemed to my outsider's eye that the rituals of observation that brought people closer to nature in Japanese culture needed the context of intimacy – places that felt safe and human in scale and that were not about a landscape that had been carved out by modern agriculture and forestry but were more in tune with the tradition of *satoyama*.

The garden masterplan

When Takano first invited me to the site, it was with the intention of adding a more intimate layer to the existing masterplan and helping to make the park more accessible to visitors. The Garden Masterplan was to be an exercise in place-making and the new destinations would aim to welcome a wider range of visitors and hold them there.

Visitor flow had already been established to a degree and it was a delight to walk the paths in the safety of the Entrance Forest, but the experience broke down at the point where people reached the restaurant that once occupied the Kisara Building. Faced with a divide created by the pasture, they were separated from the mountains by 5 hectares (12 acres) of flat, open ground. The trails that led into the woods and even to the Goat Farm, which was just a short walk across the stream, felt disconnected by this expanse of paddock. The distances were not easily defined and even with the draw of the art trail, the majority of people retraced their steps after stopping for refreshments.

Despite the presence of hot springs in the mountains, there are none on the site. If there had been, early plans for a hotel here would have been more practical, for use during the winter season when the park returns to snow. Though the Garden Masterplan reintroduced this idea (and the aspiration is still there for people to be able to stay and experience the park at dawn, sunset or during the night), the new destinations would need to work primarily for the day visitor.

My first observations were made clearer by Takano, who talked me through the principles of reconnecting people to the forest. He walked me over the site and its surroundings to see the bones of the project: the parking, the introduction to the environment in the Entrance Forest and the reveal of the mountains from the restaurant. He wanted visitors to go further, but could see that they were struggling with the scale and even a feeling of discomfort with the imposing nature of the landscape. For the public to come to love this place, and in turn develop a relationship with it that projected into the future, it was time to work another layer into the vision.

Fine-tuning a sense of place and understanding its essence is key to my work and the time spent looking at the location provided the foundations for making the right moves with the Garden Masterplan. I made several visits at different times of year to understand the place more fully, particularly to see it pared back in winter and to experience the feeling of remoteness during that season. The scale in winter, when you can see through the trees, is always different and more definable than in summer when the trees conceal much of a landscape. I visited again in the growing season, both in the spring and the late summer, to see the contrasts between the two – a landscape bristling with life, streams freshly visible to the opening of the season, then the same place consumed and dimmed once growth had reached its climax in the woodland. Summer visits revealed the need for shade and an escape from the intense sunlight out in the open. Each exploration contributed to a greater understanding of how to create places that felt appropriate and in context.

Takano took me to visit Yukihiro Izumi, a naturalist living nearby, who had already evolved a form of forest gardening that was being pioneered in Hokkaido. My first and subsequent visits proved to be a great source of personal inspiration and helped me to understand the possibilities of how to 'garden' lightly in this landscape. It also revealed to me the potential of the indigenous species, many of which were treasures to me as a foreigner. Seeing a native plant in its natural setting is a memorable experience, but Mr Izumi had drawn this into a sharp and indelible focus. Over the two decades that he had been maintaining the 8 hectares (20 acres) of the Tashiro Forest, he had evolved what he described as 'a primitive Japanese forest maintenance style'. To enable him to build upon the diversity of the species within the woods he too had cut the sasa in the autumn and, by repeating this process over five to six years, diminished the bamboo's hold on the forest floor. The short summers saw it struggle to regain complete foliage cover which, in tandem with increased light levels, triggered the perennial seedbank which had lain dormant in the leaf mould.

THE TOKACHI MILLENNIUM FOREST

1. The Entrance Forest
2. The Earth Garden
3. The Forest Garden
4. The Meadow Garden
5. Hidaka Mountains
6. Entrance

7. Parking
8. Visitor Center
9. Horse Pasture
10. Hokkaido Garden Show Site
11. Garden Café
12. Kitchen Garden

13. Rose Garden
14. Orchard
15. Goat Farm
16. Kisara Building
17. Circle of Kamui
18. Millennium Hill

1

2

3

Once the bamboo was in check, Mr Izumi 'worked' the forest with an intuitive understanding of ecology, seeding plants and relocating seedlings to places he knew they would favour. He told me that the soft and fragile-looking natives made him want to protect them from vigorous woodlanders such as *Veratrum album* subsp. *oxysepalum*, *Reynoutria japonica* (syn. *Fallopia japonica*) and *Angelica ursina*. These strong-growing species were either prevented from seeding or repeatedly cut to diminish their vigour.

Mr Izumi's practice is based on a true understanding of the woodland ecology combined with the knowledge of what he can do within the limits of his own energy. His way of 'gardening' the forest with a light and responsive hand prevents the colonization of thuggish species and gives the more aesthetically desirable species their preferred environmental niches. In so doing he has altered the balance and improved the floral content of the understorey. Developing this way of interacting with his land has allowed him to manage an 8-hectare (20-acre) site singlehandedly. The line between land management and horticulture is finely blurred, the weighting certainly being lighter on the horticulture, but his informed and continued input has resulted in a place that feels distinctly his own and particular to the Tashiro Forest.

Gardens provide a way to be closer to nature and to open up a physical dialogue through tending and nurturing an environment. I knew that some of the new spaces at the Millennium Forest would need to test the idea of what a garden was in the conventional sense. At one end of the scale, we might have a place that simply allowed the visitor to look more closely at the natural environment; a tree singled out for its unique character might interrupt a path, a seating opportunity and light clearance might suffice. We would need to tread lightly and avoid creating the feeling that we had intervened, but by heightening the experience of the woodland in a way that was particular to the Millennium Forest, we could create a stronger connection with native plants and the rhythms of the seasons. Here and there, to provide a gentle jolt of contrast, a 'gardened' place would allow people to look again with eyes reopened.

If the park were to rely upon the concept of custodianship, education would be key. Allowing visitors a deeper connection through occupying a place more wholeheartedly would, we felt, engage them more fully and encourage them to want to be part of the place quite naturally. The hope was that if we drew in a generation deeply enough they would hand the connection on to the next and, over time, a depth of feeling would develop around the place that would keep it in safe hands.

1. Dan with Fumiaki Takano and his team in June 2007 (the Meadow Garden had been constructed the year before) examining the test beds for each perennial mix prior to planting commencing 2. The site of the Meadow Garden on a visit made in 2003 3. Looking back over the Meadow Garden from the Kitchen Garden

East and west

When I first travelled to Japan in the late 1990s I went to look at the way landscape had been interpreted through the art of the garden. I saw a whole range of different gardens and the various styles that make them particular. At the most informal extreme there was the light, mostly rural hand of *satoyama* and at the other the rigour of the interpretive Zen gardens.

It was a fascinating immersion and I was struck by how important the natural world was to all the approaches to garden-making. The history of Shinto beliefs, where all living things and inanimate objects have spiritual power, played a key role in all the places I saw. A significant tree given special focus or stones carefully placed to reveal their energy provided a deeper connection to the raw materials. The natural elements were harnessed and distilled through the use of water or captured light. Seasonality was clearly expressed through the strategic use of plants so that the passage of a year was marked, each change celebrated.

Although asymmetry played an important part in the gardens I saw, the apparent informality of all the places I visited was underpinned by a deeply formal approach to composition. There were long-respected rules that articulated visitors' passage over stones in a stroll garden, the stepping stones being placed to influence both their pace and what they would focus on. Larger pausing stones offered the opportunity to take in a reveal or the wider vista of the borrowed view beyond the garden.

I found much delight in the way that the gardens helped me to be closer to the subject matter, be it the stillness of reflective water or a tree pruned in a manner to express the passage of time in its branches. It was a deep and immediate connection, but nothing had prepared me for the distance between the landscape itself and the interpretation of it in the gardens. There was always a separation from the real thing – a wall, a screen, a focused view that allowed me to see it at a distance. Few places were left unmanaged and, despite its resonance and the reverence for it, nature was held at bay and ordered into position. Although the language employed to help you see the natural world in Japan is highly sophisticated, the actual meeting point is kept at arm's length. Real nature is not invited into the garden or encouraged to run its natural course in close proximity as it might be in the gardens of the West.

A fundamental objective of the Garden Masterplan was to provide people with a way into the natural environment that was easy, familiar and unthreatening. I wanted to draw upon the garden being a meeting place between the ordered world of man and the apparently unordered world of nature – a comfortable place where the hand of man is in evidence and there are recognizable moments that help provide intimacy. My foreigner's take on making a garden here would benefit from the outsider's eye. I wanted to make a place that drew upon the Japanese art of garden-making fused with a northern European understanding of *genius loci* while introducing a looser European naturalism then unfamiliar in Japan. I wanted to invite nature in to the managed places and for one to speak to the other.

My first port of call with any project is always to walk the site with a view to understanding its essence. From these close observations of the way things grow and the elemental qualities that are particular to a place, a direction can be established that has an immediate connection to its surroundings. What I was keen to do at the Millennium Forest was to find a way of bringing the cultural differences together. We would celebrate the water and the woods in the Entrance Forest and draw its seasonality into focus. We would abstract the foothills in the Earth Garden and so borrow the spectacle of the mountains, as one might with the traditional practice of *shakkei,* the borrowed view. The familiar ways of reading landscape through the Japanese garden would be brought close in the trails that actually made their way into these compositions.

In the Productive Gardens we would draw upon the concept of *satoyama* and the familiarity of living off the land, while in the Meadow Garden we would bring the whole experience together with a planting that looked to naturalism as its guide. The paths in the garden would feel like the trails in the woodland, pushing close and moving through a whole environment. We would cross water to enter the garden with the protection of the woods to one side and the grandeur of the mountains as the borrowed view. The planting would be immersive and take its lead from the communities of native plants, but heighten the experience through combining plants in a free and painterly manner.

Naturalistic planting was completely new in Japan at this stage, but we felt sure that we could use the garden to open people's eyes to a way of gardening that respected nature and pushed against it only lightly – a way that was closer to the old ways, of knowing where food was to be found in the woods and managing the plants that grew there for our benefit. It felt entirely possible that we could make a garden at the Millennium Forest that would in some ways feel not foreign but familiar. We could invite nature closer here and provide a distilled way of seeing the natural world through the garden feeling part of the place – tuned and heightened by horticultural intervention, but relating directly to the local culture and being part of its surroundings.

A year in planning and five years of implementation

Time and again, my first impressions on site are the things I come back to during the design process. Whether it's the good things that strike me immediately or the knots and awkwardnesses of a place, both the good and the bad have to be examined and weighed. Despite the conundrums that were presented to me here, I could see very quickly where the site had drama and a richness of opportunity. The ecology of the regenerating forest floor was remarkable and a fundamental source of inspiration. I knew that all the answers for how to make the design lay in understanding the language of the context.

I travelled back to the UK during that first year of visits in 2000 with photographs of the site and pages of notes capturing my observations and feelings. The notes referred to the secluded places and where the best views were to be had and where the atmosphere needed to be honed to make it more legible and tangible. Seasonal studies recorded where the plants followed the water in the forest or showed a preference for open places or free-draining knolls. Although not a strict botanical survey, these on-the-ground observations were key for they allowed me to 'read' the land and understand its potential. I looked at the rhythm of growth and how, over the course of the year, one layer superseded the next. This helped me to understand the interdependency of

Overleaf: Native *Hemerocallis esculenta* can be found flowering in the forest in late June.

the plants and the range of material that already grew there. Observing the way the native plants inhabited the site helped me to establish which places already had resonance and what the new places would be, driven by what grew there.

The Garden Masterplan, which was drawn up back in London, detailed a narrative of cohesive experiences that would be appropriate to their setting and meaningful as a way of illustrating something specific about that place. The range of experiences were all set within the context of a walk that would reveal the park in an intimate way as the visitor moved through it. I knew we would need to play with scale and do that with confidence, and there should be boldness in contrast to the intimacy in the placemaking. A key move, for instance, would be to bridge the gap between the Entrance Forest and the mountains. The open ground that separated these two worlds would need to become a landscape that you could imagine walking into and that would provide an intuitive move onward, up towards the mountains and into the wilder forest on one side and, on the other, to a safe and tended garden.

The Entrance Forest formed the introduction and a way to look closely at woodland flora, carefully managed to enhance its diversity and floral impact. I wanted to open a view from the restaurant to connect the distant view more definitely with a new landform that would bring the mountains closer. The paddocks to the left that connected to the goat farm would become the site for a new garden that had as its boundaries the new landforms, the edge of woodland, a mountain view and the goat farm. This garden would reinterpret the woodland floor in the form of a naturalistic meadow. The merits of naturalistic gardening were new to Japan and I envisaged the new Meadow Garden would provide a place to look again at the natural world and how we can nurture it through horticulture.

Beyond the Meadow Garden, to anchor the farm buildings, I planned a series of gardens that would have practicality and production at their core. A kitchen garden with vegetables, herbs, fruit and a cutting garden would illustrate the principles of growing to eat and growing organically. An orchard would show the range of fruits that could be cultivated this far north. In the original Garden Masterplan, the Rose Farm extended into the agricultural fields to complement the Goat Farm with rose-derived products, while a petting area would allow visitors a closer connection to the goats and their presence on the land.

The Garden Masterplan was presented to Mr Hayashi in 2003 and work began the next year with the grand gesture of the Earth Garden. From there, taking on one to two projects a year, we followed through with the Meadow Garden, the Farm Garden and Menagerie, the Rose Garden and the Orchard.

Midori and the team

Midori Shintani arrived at the Millennium Forest in the spring of 2008, in time to prepare the soil and plant the Meadow Garden for the official opening. The task of communicating the ethos of the gardens was made easier by her understanding of the Western approach to gardening and her background enabled her to easily bridge the cultural differences. Midori learned English when she was sent to study with a Dutch family near her hometown in Honshu. Her parents' aim was to teach her a modern duality that immersed her in the Western sensibility and then, when she was at home, she would learn the Japanese ways. Her grandfather was a strong influence and he taught her about the tradition of the tea ceremony, kimono, ceramics and literature. She refers to this time as 'a period of opposites'.

Midori left home early, and after studying formal Japanese horticulture and landscape architecture at Minami Kyushu University, Japan, she worked as a landscaper to learn the practicalities of the art and the stern ethos of the way that things are done. To become a Master Gardener in Japan, the training is strict and slow, often taking as long as 25 years. As a consequence, the art of being a gardener is a respected discipline that is as much philosophical as it is practical.

Knowing she wanted her horizons to be broad and to embrace the Western part of her upbringing, in 2002 Midori journeyed to Sweden to work as a student gardener, first at Millesgården and then at Rosendals Trädgård in Stockholm, where she learnt about biodynamic horticulture – contrasting cultures again, but an education that has allowed us to find commonality between our two very different ways of gardening.

We were quickly at ease on first meeting, thanks to Midori's fluency in English and understanding of Western nuance. I liked her openness immediately, as well as her strength and humility. After walking her through the areas that had already been realized from the Garden Masterplan, we ventured into the forest. I wanted to explain how, by observing the natural ecosystems in the forest, we would find a way to tend the gardens naturalistically. We stood in a clearing amid the layering of summer perennials and I talked her through the way I saw the planting being an echo of the natural sequences and interdependencies. We looked around us to take in the environment and then through the layers, from the ascending aralia down through the mingling of filipendula and thalictrum and the fine lines of the sedges. We parted the foliage and found underneath, already going into dormancy, an earlier spring layer of trillium, anemone and primula all in balance and each in its own niche. I explained that all the answers lay here in the forest and that the way things grew together was our guide. It wasn't a long conversation, but at the end of it she said, 'I think I understand,' and I responded with, 'I know that you do.'

A designer's role is as much about a vision for a place as it is the physical manifestation of a design process. A gardener's role is vital to the day-to-day realization of that vision and the relationship between designer and gardener is fundamental for the ideas to have a future. Midori has been totally committed to the vision. She has understood that, though we are pioneering the Western approach to naturalistic planting, we are also making a garden that is appropriate to this place; to the forest and the wild places and to the managed land and the agriculture. There is a direct and appropriate way of doing things here and her knowledge of *satoyama* has been fundamental in bringing our two worlds together. It was a relief to know that the risk I had taken in making a garden that was designed to be lightly steered would be in a safe pair of hands, ones that were used to juggling both cultures and finding the common ground.

I return once a year to the Millennium Forest at different times in the growing season to workshop the garden and its direction with Midori. This is always a fascinating process, seeing the garden through Midori's eyes and hearing her knowledge of the garden day-to-day revealed in conversation. We are joined now by Shintaro Sasagawa, Assistant Head Gardener and invaluable member of the team, and together we identify the strengths and weaknesses and where to apply energies for the year ahead. Maintaining such a range of habitats with a limited work force is not without its challenges and dictates the need for focus. The 2016 typhoon, for instance, took more than a year to recover from and the extreme climate dictates a need to work with ingenuity and speed in the spring and the autumn.

Midori aspires to a team of four but a core team of three is usually the norm, because she has to strip back to three for winter and rehiring in such a remote location is a challenge. Part-time workers help with specific manual tasks at peak points in the year, doing weeding, woodland work and some of the repairs, but not all, for Midori uses her landscaping skills where she can. In the summer months Midori also accepts one or two carefully vetted student gardeners from overseas who want to learn the ways of tending this place. In addition to the cultural and horticultural cross-fertilization that this encourages, it extends the educational reach of the forest.

For several years we have been operating an exchange between Great Dixter, home of the late Christopher Lloyd, and the Millennium Forest. Midori's team travel in the winter to garden in the UK during this productive time, while in the summer Head Gardener Fergus Garrett has sent members of his team to the Millennium Forest. The exchange has been rich and informative, with both the head and assistant gardeners exchanging experiences and expertise. Despite their highly different gardening styles the two gardens have more in common than one might expect, for the juxtaposition of good horticulture and a connection to the local ecology are believed to be essential in both gardens.

We are lucky that Mr Hayashi sees the benefit in my coming to the forest every year. He understands that the time Midori and I spend together, be it only a few days, is invaluable. Over the years we have also taken some time for ourselves, travelling together to look at other landscapes, places and people that inspire. We have delighted in our cultural cross-overs and differences and our alliance is manifested in the way that the garden grows.

Opposite, above: Assistant Head Gardener, Shintaro Sasagawa, Dan Pearson and Head Gardener, Midori Shintani, in the Meadow Garden on one of the annual maintenance visits. *Below:* Dan at the 10th anniversary celebration of the Tokachi Millennium Forest in July 2018 with Mitsushige Hayashi, Hiroshi Hayashi and Katsuhiko Hayashi.

Overleaf: On the left, the distinctive leaves of *Magnolia obovata*, a primary component of the native Tokachi Millennium Forest. They are used as serving platters and to wrap slow cooked meat.

THE FOREST

The long-term vision

The forest is the metaphor for longevity in the naming of the park. It predates the arrival of humans here and will ultimately remain the constant, but since the island was colonized at the end of the 19th century it has gone through considerable change. Logging in the early 1900s removed the most mature oak and where the ground was not replanted with larch for logging, the regeneration has seen a shift in the ecology. Pioneer species such as birch and willow made their way in first and fast, but the slower-growing species such as the oaks and the magnolias have had to battle with the sasa. This invasive bamboo travels quickly when light levels are opened up and it is strong enough to hold a monocultural grip over other species, which is only eased when shade from taller trees once again becomes the dominant presence. It takes generations for this to happen.

Managing the forest for greater diversity and a balanced ecology has been part of the long-term vision, but a site as large as the Millennium Forest can only be managed in part and very lightly on the whole. If one imagines a series of ripples from a stone cast into water, the greater energy is applied to the areas designated for the casual visitor. This includes the Entrance Forest, the Meadow Garden, the Earth Garden and the Productive Gardens. Secondary ripples include the site of the Hokkaido Garden Show and a circular walk that now extends into the horse paddocks. It also includes an area called the Forest Garden where a site of previous habitation is explored by a work by Takano Landscape Planning and where the forest floor is being gently managed to improve diversity. Tertiary ripples include trails up onto the open ground of the immediate foothills and deeper into the forest where the riding routes are kept open by foresters, but come with a bear warning.

The Entrance Forest and the gently managed woodland

As you enter the shadows of the Entrance Forest the mountains are hidden from view, though they are still fresh in your memory from the drive to the Millennium Forest. Despite the wild and untouched feeling, much has been done to make this place feel gentle and welcoming. It gives the visitor the opportunity to meet the forest in a safe and intimate setting that is perhaps more easy to adjust to than the wilder places that make the later chapters on the journey.

While passing through here you are sheltered by the trees, which provide a feeling of calm and stillness. Gateway stones, which sit heavily within the vegetation to either

Opposite: The boardwalks in the Entrance Forest allow visitors a light footfall on the woodland floor and close proximity to the surroundings.

Overleaf: The diversity of vegetation in the Entrance Forest was made possible by strimming the dominant sasa and gently steering the native vegetation for greatest diversity. Here the pink flowers of *Filipendula glaberrima* (ezo-no-shimotsukeso) and the white plumes of *Aruncus dioicus* var. *camschaticus* (yamabukishoma) in early July.

side of the path, are placed to mark the point of arrival. A network of paths inclines gently towards the mountains, taking you close to the flow of a rushing stream. Some are raised wooden walkways which pass over water and keep the visitor elevated, others are soft bark paths that follow the contours and push closer to the plants. The paths are designed to slow and retune the senses and provide visitors with the comfort of a well-defined passage into the woodland.

The terrain of the Entrance Forest forms a shallow valley that rises slowly away and a fast-running stream switches to either side of the entrance woodland energizing the place. An easy route takes the high flank to the left and comes close to an area of sasa which has been deliberately left unmanaged, so that it buffers the boundary. As you look down from this path to the low ground alongside you, particularly in spring when the vegetation is low, you can see an alternative route that engages with the stream.

The dip where the stream rushes is the natural point of focus and the more immersive route starts with an earth path that breaks away from the easy path near its beginning and moves towards the sound of water. It passes closely through tree trunks clad with *Hydrangea petiolaris* and up onto a raised wooden walkway that leads to the other side of the woodland and towards the light. An open glade backdropped by wooded foothills reveals paddocks where horses graze just beyond the trees. The path then switches back again across the water to take in more of the dappled environment. From the walkway you can look down upon the woodland floor and be close to it without inflicting the damage of footfall. In the wet places you might see a huddle of emerald green skunk cabbage. In summer the enormous paddle-shaped leaves combine with finely drawn sedges and the parasols of *Petasites japonicus* subsp. *giganteus* to give little away of the caltha and anemone that preceded them. In the drier parts, and where the trees are slung with roping vines of actinidia, stands of *Cardiocrinum cordatum* var. *glehnii* rise up through *Aconitum sachalinense* subsp. *yezoense*, from which the Ainu made poison for their arrows when hunting bears.

Aside from the paths it is difficult today to discern the careful calculations that were made to heighten the mood here more than 20 years ago. Following clearance of the sasa, first steps included a gentle thinning of the existing trees, involving on-the-ground selection to define a route for the paths and to open up glades to allow the eye to travel within the woodland. The thinning process was also designed to allow light to fall to the forest floor in differing intensities to encourage diversity in the woodland perennials.

Under Midori's careful guidance there has been an ongoing practice of refinement in the approach to managing the Entrance Forest so that over time it has developed its own distinctive atmosphere. Gentle management keeps the upper hand over the sasa and responds to the natural flux that happens as conditions make themselves conducive to particular species. This might be a tree falling and changing the light levels or a storm that washes clear new ground to expose a pioneer position in the ecology. Encouraging natural regeneration requires close observation and opening up the best opportunities for the plants to succeed as a community.

Opposite: Aconitum sachalinense subsp. yezoense (ezo-torikabuto), one of many native treasures that occupy their own particular niche in the Entrance Forest.

Cardiocrinum cordatum var. glehnii (o-ubayuri)

Aruncus dioicus var. camschaticus (yamabukishoma)

Anemone flaccida (nirinso)

Many of these genera are familiar to gardeners, but the species are often either endemic to the Japanese archipelago or to Hokkaido alone.

Primula jesoana (o-sakuraso)

Glaucidium palmatum (shiraneaoi)

Caltha palustris var. barthei (ezo-no-ryukinka), *Symplocarpus foetidus* (zazenso) and emerging *Veratrum album* subsp. *oxysepalum* (baikeiso)

Corydalis ambigua (ezoengosaku)

Paris verticillata (kurumaba-tsukubaneso)

Overleaf: The native butterbur *Petasites japonicus* subsp. *giganteus* (akitabuki) proliferates in the wet hollows, emerging early in spring and foraged for young shoots. Here it is fully grown with *Thalictrum minus* var. *hypoleucum* (aki-karamatsu) later in summer.

Veratrum album subsp. *oxysepalum* (baikeiso)

Lysimachia europaea (tsumatoriso)

Arisaema serratum (koraitennansho)

Aquilegia oxysepala (oyama-odamaki)

Aconitum gigas (ezo-no-reijinso)

Lilium medeoloides (kurumayuri)

Filipendula glaberrima (ezo-no-shimotsukeso)

Hypericum ascyron (tomoeso)

Veratrum maackii (syuroso)

Thalictrum baicalense (haru-karamatsu)

Hosta sieboldii var. *rectifolia* (tachi-giboshi)

Osmundastrum cinnamomeum (yamadori-zenmai)

Overleaf: The sasa clearance in the Forest Garden
is an annual task. By curbing its hold on the forest floor
the diversity of native species returns from the
seedbank beneath the leaf mould.

Certain plants such as fallopia are retained on the margins as examples of wild forage plants. Colonies of already existing perennials are improved by allowing them their reign where they favour a particular position. It is a year-on-year process that has allowed this area of the forest to reveal its plants to visitors, who sense the heightened mood but are not aware of the minimal intervention.

Though the hand of the gardener becomes increasingly less appropriate in the forest that lies further into the park, a gentle steer is practised wherever a place needs to feel more comfortable. Streamside walks, crossings made with boulders and wilder places are made to feel easier by the localized clearance of sasa and the resulting shift in the balance allows the eye to travel in the woodland and for there to be a sense of prospect. The interventions are all but invisible to the untrained eye, but very much felt and conducive to the visitor feeling less out of place in nature and more a part of the forest. Every spring, soon after snowmelt and once the first plants are visible, Midori and her team put a burst of energy into 'improving' the forest floor. It is timely, for this is the first activity after a long winter and it is good then to engage with the first signs of life. The approach is modulated in the areas of the forest that are attended to and work extends to the site of the Hokkaido Garden Show and across the stream to the Forest Garden. Here, where the sasa was more recently cleared and the flora is yet to be as rich as the Entrance Forest, there is a more directly applied approach to managing the perennial layer. Lysichiton and other plants of spectacle such as *Glaucidium palmatum* are transplanted from the forest nursery to improve colonies in the spring. To save energies, a more relaxed regime is employed throughout the summer to keep paths clear and invasive species in check. They are otherwise maintained with minimal intervention. Midori harbours near invisible 'nurseries' in the forest. They are not open to the public but she carries out a careful from of husbandry here to rear the native plants, which are encouraged to increase directly where they have chosen to be and can be left to tick over while maturing. Seedlings are also kept in these woodland nurseries and, when they are ready, splits and divisions are taken and moved to build upon the natural plant communities that show that they have found a place that indicates the right conditions.

Forest foraging is an important part of this early activity in spring and there are areas that are deep in the forest where Midori and her team go to harvest food for the garden café. They wear bear-bells around their waists when doing so as they are not the only creatures in the forest that are pining for the nutritious bitterness of first growth. The bears are hungry when they come out of hibernation in the spring and are often looking for the same forage material or plants, which they use as a post-hibernation purgative. This process of living from the awakening land reminds the team that there has been a long relationship with manipulating the forest both for food and building materials. Time spent harvesting is also time observing and evaluating what moves need to be made to strike a balance with the forest.

Right: A solitary *Trillium tschonoskii* (miyama-enreiso) alongside unfurling *Matteuccia struthiopteris* (kusasotetsu). The pleated foliage of *Veratrum album* subsp. *oxysepalum* (baikeiso) in the background.

Overleaf: A stand of native plants on the forest margin includes the distinctive shield-shaped foliage of *Fallopia sachalinensis* (o-itadori), whose shoots and young stems are edible, and emerging *Cirsium kamtschaticum* (chishima-azami).

Midori Shintani

Hands for the forest

Hokkaido is the land of pioneers. The land of the Tokachi Millennium Forest also has its history. When the first pioneers arrived at Tokachi Shimizu 120 years ago, I have heard that 13 families lived in this forest once. Since then, the forest has been reclaimed over and over as people have changed hands. Under the harsh nature of Hokkaido, reclamation would have been a series of difficulties. Every time a blizzard rages from the Hidaka Mountains in winter, I see the pasture on the hill once cultivated by the pioneers and imagine the severity of their lives.

The last farmer here left the land due to having no successors, and so the forest was left abandoned for more than 20 years, until the Hayashi family arrived. The second pioneering began with the carbon offset project of their newspaper business. Then the garden project launched with Takano Landscape Planning, the development of which is ongoing with Dan and many people today. The forest has been watching all these frontier-lines.

Our forest stewardship is diverse. Apart from the gardens, 270 hectares (667 acres) of the site consists of multi-layered forests of coniferous and deciduous trees, single-layered larch forests, and the area converting single-layered forests into multi-layered forests. On this forestry site, we are also developing effective uses of the forest such as native plant nurseries, forage forests, nature guided tour areas and horse pastures.

The annual forest management is planned by the Shimizu Forestry Association, the Tokachi Mainichi Newspaper and the Tokachi Millennium Forest. I joined the forest stewardship team in 2010, taking over from my predecessors. We carry out forest management by thinning, improvement-cutting, weeding and

Midori in a relaxed area of the forest where the sasa is less rigorously controlled.

In spring, Midori and her team add to the
communities of native plants in the forest by splitting
and transplanting. This is a colony of
Lysichiton camtschatcensis (mizubasho).

sweeping including areas of the Entrance Forest, the Forest Garden and the Hokkaido Garden Show site. Forest stewardship is the cornerstone for all our activities in the Millennium Forest.

The Forest Garden, designed by Takano Landscape Planning, has a rich vegetation of oaks (*Quercus mongolica* subsp. *crispula*). Interesting signs of pioneers' life remain in this forest, such as trees coppiced about 100 years ago and a field eroded by birches (*Betula platyphylla*) which tells a history of cultivation for housing or farming.

The Entrance Forest is a symbolic place that allows us to realize that we all share one nature. We nurture native plants and introduce them to visitors here. Our methods of forest-floor maintenance are to rejuvenate the seed bank in the soil by strimming the vigorous sasa which dominates the ground, collecting seeds and returning seedlings to the forest, and transplanting from other areas to the Forest Garden and the Hokkaido Garden Show site. The vegetation had been nurtured by our previous 'pioneer' staff since 1990 when the forest wasn't even named yet.

I and my team took over this forest-floor maintenance from our predecessors during 2008 and 2009. The approach at that time was focused on tackling some specific undesirable species. During those years I monitored the wild habitats of Tokachi, such as seaside meadows, mountain vegetation and marshlands, and also the various levels of manipulation in private forests and meadows. Once I found a unique camping site where the land management stimulated the native vegetation. The forest floor of this camping site was cut back to keep it clean for campers to set up their tents during summer. As this yearly process was repeated, the number of the plants such as *Anemone flaccida*, *Corydalis cordata* and *Trillium camschatcense* increased, and formed a colony in the spring. When these spring ephemerals have dropped seed and vanished from the ground in June, the camping season starts and the ground is maintained by cutting back the other vegetation in readiness for the campers. Use of the site by people brings a great opportunity for the spring ephemerals to expand their vegetation without competition in summer. People also enjoy seeing these beautiful flowers in spring. The rich vegetation is often well protected, but as a gardener who works to draw out the charm of the place, I find it interesting when plants and humans share a place in this way.

Through these experiences I positively questioned and reconsidered how our forest stewardship should be. Since 2010, we have articulated our forest-floor stewardship policy, clarified the purpose of each area of the forest and reviewed seasonal tasks. In the Forest Garden, it is important to harmonize the relationship between native plants and the garden design of resting spaces, boulder settings and watersides. We keep managing conventional methods of planting seedlings, transplanting and encouraging desirable plants by thinning the others in the spring and the summer. Sometimes intensive hands are needed in this garden to reduce wild animal damage.

On the other hand, I realized that the Entrance Forest has rich layers of flora and high potential for its own dynamism regardless of environmental factors. By our hands of manipulating and gardening, we had been losing a precious opportunity to see, as closely as possible, the natural vegetation of the forest. We changed direction to minimal manipulation. We cut the sasa back once in the autumn and exterminate only invasive alien species such as *Solidago gigantea* and *Rudbeckia laciniata* as early as possible in the spring and the summer so as not to damage the vegetation. As a result, the Entrance Forest has gradually begun to form its own remarkable rhythm and balance of plant communities.

The Entrance Forest has been reborn as a valuable place for visitors, gardeners and everyone in the Millennium Forest to learn about the character of native plants and to understand the effects of environmental changes through the natural vegetation and its transitions. When the typhoon struck the Millennium Forest in 2016, the forest floor of the Entrance Forest was flooded by the overflowing stream, like washing away the past. It goes without saying that we held our breath to watch the plants the following year and celebrated their reunion and evolution.

An augmented colony of
Lysichiton camtschatcensis in the
Forest Garden.

THE EARTH GARDEN

A place between the forest and the mountains

The Earth Garden was the first of the projects to be realized and the catalyst for a dramatic change to the Millennium Forest. The action of making it demonstrated the tremendous confidence of Mr Hayashi and signalled a definite commitment to bringing the park to life. It was also the largest earth-forming project that I had yet realized and a time of great excitement (and some trepidation) about seeing the first part of the Garden Masterplan come to life.

When I first saw the site, it was clear that all the magic that had been captured in the Entrance Forest was lost as soon as the paths exited the woodland. The restaurant was the destination here and the building had been placed on the very edge of a 5-hectare (2 1/2-acre) paddock with a breathtaking panorama of the mountains. The transition from the shelter and intimacy of the forest was jolting and sudden. The open ground, which was the result of earlier agricultural clearance, symbolized an intimidating gulf between the forest and the mountains and the flat, featureless ground made it impossible to register scale, which was borne out in visitors simply not venturing further.

From the shelter of the restaurant you could see the Circle of Kamui, a monumental circle of stones by sculptor Masaru Bando which marked the gateway to the mountain. A trail to Millennium Hill, the nearest foothill, exited the paddock at this point and though in reality the distances were not far, it was only the intrepid who made their way across the expanse of open ground. To either side of the paddock raced fast-moving streams that brought snowmelt from the mountain. If you made your way to the streams, you found intimacy again and the comfort of being part of something more human in scale. You could imagine the Ainu working the streams for fish, the shelter of the alder and willow providing shade and a buffer from the mountain winds.

Shakkei, the principle of incorporating a borrowed view, is a thing of great subtlety in Japanese landscape gardens, but when the mountains were on show in clear weather they were almost overwhelming in their intensity. Without a foreground or introduction that felt more intimate, they also appeared remote and unattainable. I wanted to bring the mountains closer and for this to be somewhere that welcomed the visitor and provided a sense of discovery and connection.

I walked the land to see how the far ridges appeared in relation to the nearest feature of Millennium Hill. The break with the horizontal provided by this foothill provided an important middle distance and, once my eye became attuned, it soon revealed other hills that were similar in form and framed the paddock where the horses grazed to the east.

In winter the landforms are reduced to their purest form of light and shadow.

Key site lines were captured on a contour map that defined the ground and allowed me to see its boundaries. I recorded how the light fell through the space at different times of day and imagined it being intercepted rather than falling flatly into the empty arena. I made movements to, through and from the paddock in sketch form and captured the near and the far distance in a series of panoramic photographs so that I could bring my written notes together with a visual record in the studio in London.

The studies were to support my immediate impression, which was that the paddock should be the site of a dramatic new land form, one that would make the connection between the forest and the mountain with a series of sensual undulations. The sculpted ground would capture the elements – the light falling and the wind that raced across it – while grounding and sheltering the restaurant with a dynamic foreground that was enticing and invited exploration.

Back in the studio, I sketched the horizon lines, both near and far, and noted the difference between the soft foothills and the dramatic horizon of the Hidaka Mountains. Looking more closely at the topographical map, it became clear that a ridge that ran through the middle of the site was more significant than it had felt when I was on the ground. Such is the play of scale, for the open ground had disguised the ridge, which ran from front to back and fell gently to the streams to either side. It became clear on paper that this rise in the ground would have to be the starting point for the landforms, like the swell that provides the energy of a wave. The streams, the restaurant and the gateway to the hills provided by Masaru Bando's artwork were our other fixed points. We also needed to consider how the landform could help to provide lateral movements into the forest to the right and the site of the proposed Meadow Garden to the left. The earthwork would have to work on a grand scale to connect the mountains to the foreground and on a small scale to steer people towards where we wanted them to be.

To allow the space to register on a more definable scale I drew a series of ridges on the plan, like waves coming into shore. I imagined myself at the restaurant site with the undulations rolling towards me to bring the surge of the mountains closer in a series of moderated foothills. As this is a 5-hectare (12-acre) site the scale was still huge, so the forms were made up to 8m (26ft) high in places from peak to trough. Drawn flat on a plan they appeared like folds in a sheet, some concave, others convex, creating places between them where you could imagine moving in the hollows or rising to a peak for orientation.

The plans from my studio in London were sent to Takano's office in Hokkaido so that a 1:20 scale model could be made in sand and the space tested. The model, complete with miniature rakes so that the forms could be adjusted, was set out in the yard of the old schoolhouse where his practice is based. There is nothing quite like a model to test an idea and it allowed us to see that a number of the forms would be better pulled closer together by the stream to intensify the experience as the visitor crossed it there.

Once I was happy with the configuration and it was signed off in principle, Takano's office went through the lengthy process of testing the viability of the earthworks on the

1. Dan surveys the site of the Earth Garden in October 2004, prior to ground works commencing 2. A sketch of the proposed Earth Garden 3. An early paper model

1

2

3

1

2

3

4

ground. The landforms would be created using a cut and fill exercise, with the height of each wave formed half by the cut into the ground and half by the mound made upon the cut. However, we needed to find out if we could dig in the first place. Test holes were dug across the site to see if the ridge was in fact a seam of rock. It was, but as we had already allowed for this as a swell in the landform, it was accommodated in a rise that formed one of the waves. The test holes also revealed that it was possible to dig where we needed to with minor adjustment, but a subterranean water system moved extensively through the ground and this would need to be drained.

We could not have made the project work from a distance had it not been for the technical input of Takano's team, who drew up the details for constructing the excavations and draining them and also managed the works. I returned more than once before the earthwork was complete to find a number of bulldozers active on the site. It was immensely exciting to see the idea, sketches and plans becoming three-dimensional and so much more monumental than I had ever imagined. The forms reared up over the course of a season and then spent the winter buried under snow before being hydroseeded in the spring. A mixture of paper pulp and grass seed was sprayed onto the steepest slopes to stabilize the inclines, while the rolls between them were seeded conventionally.

The experience now

As the forms greened, the upheaval became absorbed into the landscape. Though I had imagined the ground being changed by the earthwork and had, I thought, comprehended the scale of what we were doing, it was a surprise to find the experience of being in this new place to be bigger in every way. The mountains were drawn closer and appeared in more detail with the new landform echoing their glory in the foreground. The restaurant was held by the landform and, with the new prospect, you were immediately drawn into the undulating ground to make your way towards the mountains. The new space worked hard, providing a setting for the spectacle of the borrowed view and inspiring a sense of discovery.

The Earth Garden was named after completion, as we felt it needed a name that had sufficient gravity to match the experience of being there. Walking it is a completely three-dimensional experience and a surprise, initially, for the way it sharpens your senses. The concave forms give the impression that they are enfolding you and, standing at the base of a slope rising steeply behind you, the intensity of the mountains is brought into focus, like a seashell amplifying sound; you feel the weight and stillness of the mountains and register their details more acutely. Move between the undulations to position yourself at the base of a convex form and the sound of the streams to either side is channelled and intensified. The view here is expanded, the mountains suddenly closer than they were before, but seen once again in panorama.

1. Looking down from Millennium Hill to survey the extent of the landforms during construction in November 2005 2. To create the landforms, earth was moved from an excavated cut to an area of fill. The cut and fill come together to double the resulting height 3. The landforms were deliberately designed to play with scale and humble the visitor 4. The steep slopes were hydroseeded (sprayed with paper pulp mixed with seed) directly onto the soil in spring. The pulp holds the seed in place while it germinates and gets a foothold.

Overleaf: The shallow inclines are mown close and carefully maintained for a velvety appearance. Their stillness marks a contrast with the long grass on the steep slopes, which captures the wind moving across the Earth Garden.

Above, left: The soft roll of the foothills is drawn close by the landform and encourages the eye to travel, instilling a sense of limitless boundaries. *Right:* The elemental nature of the seasons is made acute in the landforms.

Overleaf: The unification of snow, light and shadow.

It is profound to feel so small within the Earth Garden, but the feeling is not one of being lost, as it was in the expanse of the open paddocks. The physical reaction is hard to measure, for it puts demands upon your spatial awareness, but when I walk the garden a period of acclimatization always happens that leaves me feeling that I have been through a process of recalibration. When this experience is over, I feel fully in the place and part of something that is altogether bigger than we are.

The waves encourage movement and a sense of passage. You are drawn to meander, to allow the landform to steer you either between its flanks and shoulders or up to gain prospect at a crest. The experience from every rise has its own quality and similarly the troughs have their own sense of journey. Some lead your eye to a framed and distant view, others to a crossing over the stream made clear by gentle direction. It is intriguing to watch this happen and witness children in the space, fearless and followed by their parents who naturally pursue and then find themselves unlocking the network of places that exist between the rises and falls. It is at one moment a place of energy, discovery and excitement or, if you find yourself alone, another of peace, contemplation and gravity.

The grasses of the steep slopes are left to grow long in the summer so that the wind can be charted in their movement. The velvety contours of the closely cropped turf on the rolling ground allow the light to fall with greater or lesser intensity on the flanks. I have been there at the beginning of winter with sleet skidding over the forms revealing the wind flow as in a wind tunnel. Midori has sent me images of the Earth Garden deep in the winter 'with snow whipped like meringues'. It is a place that has surprised us all by intensifying the power of the elements around it and bringing them together: earth, mountain, water, forest and light.

Opposite, above: In the depth of winter the landforms take on their most sculptural presence. *Below:* In mist and with the heavy cloud of the rainy season, the Earth Garden becomes an autonomous landscape. The distant view no longer plays a part.

Overleaf: Pumpkin 'Rouge Vif d'Etampes', one of the classic heirloom varieties grown in the Kitchen Garden.

THE PRODUCTIVE GARDENS

Connecting people and the land

The Hokkaido Garden Path is a tourist initiative that makes a link between eight contemporary gardens on the island and has been pivotal in bringing more visitors to the park. At the Millennium Forest, the Productive Gardens offer a traditional view of horticulture which gives them a way into the more challenging naturalistic parts of the park.

The Tokachi Millennium Forest sits at the meeting point of the agricultural plains and the forest, so it was necessary for our approach to relate to human endeavour in both areas. Until the early 1900s the indigenous Ainu hunted and gathered by working the rivers and the hunting grounds of the meadows and forests. Today modern agriculture and forestry plays a significant role in the island economy. In domesticating today's relationship with the land in Hokkaido and scaling it down to make a garden, we were able to reintroduce the principle of *satoyama*. This ancient tradition of living in harmony with nature is completely appropriate to the way the park is run and helps to make a Western design accessible to Japanese visitors. The homestead is represented by the Garden Café and the Goat Farm; close by we have the Kitchen Garden where food is grown to eat, while, within a stone's throw, the forest provides opportunities to forage for food and materials.

In the West we are excited by the apparent newness of eating seasonally, buying food that is regional and locally sourced and foraging for food in the wild. In truth, we are just a couple of generations removed from this reality being commonplace. In Japan, eating seasonally is completely natural, as is the sense of place being on your plate, but modernization and Westernization have created a degree of separation there too. Regardless of culture, the fork-to-fork principle of knowing where your food comes from and seeing it growing alongside you is core to our message of being close to the land and caring for it.

Where agriculture excludes people due to mechanization and its complete control of an environment, the hands-on act of horticulture provides a more intimate and accessible way into the natural world. With its cool climate, Hokkaido has also become home to a new style of gardening that looks to the West rather than its own more formal tradition of garden-making. The gardens that have horticulture visibly at their core also help as a bridge between the order of a tended garden and the lighter, but still nurturing, hand in the naturalistic areas. Make the connection between the act of nurturing your environment for productivity and it is just a small step to seeing the forest and its hinterlands as a place of plenty.

Opposite: Companion planting salad in the kitchen garden. The first crop of the season.

Overleaf: The apple orchard experiments with cold-tolerant varieties. After planting, clover was introduced into the grass mix to help fix nitrogen to assist with the establishment of the trees. Camassia were added later to provide spring interest.

Pages 122-3: The stock beds are an essential element of the working part of the gardens and allow for experimentation, trials of new plants and propagation. They sit close to the greenhouse and the goat pen so that the public get a sense of what goes on behind the scenes.

The Kitchen Garden

In contrast to the informality of the Meadow Garden that adjoins it, the Kitchen Garden is designed to illustrate horticulture at play in a practical and informative setting. In line with all the gardening at the Millennium Forest, the Kitchen Garden is gardened organically. A formal system of raised beds helps to frame the experience that surrounds the Garden Café and provides an ordered means of growing produce. Midori and her team instigate a different planting plan every year, rotating the herbs, vegetables and the flowers for cutting. New plants are put on trial and grown in different ways to illustrate intercropping, companion planting, staking and harvesting, while Western varieties are mixed with Japanese vegetables to capture both a feeling of abundance and the meeting point of the two cultures in gardening.

The Garden Café is the heart of the Productive Gardens. Produce from the garden and foraged wild food from the forest are both on the menu and you can eat inside or out on a terrace shaded by indigenous kiwi vine (*Actinidia arguta*). Go into the woods and you can see these vines roping through the trees. Though the fruits are known to encourage the bears in the autumn, so far the animals have kept to the forest. Yamasachi grapes, grafted onto the roots of the wild grapes that were once eaten by the Ainu, also continue to make a link with Hokkaido's past.

To the side of the Garden Café, a covered terrace provides a sheltered place for an evolving table display which marks the shifts in the season. The still lifes that Midori and her team create here are in constant flux and bring the richness of all the areas of the park together. Wild plants from the forest, cultivated flowers, fruits and vegetables are juxtaposed to capture the moment and allow for close observation.

The *Malus sieboldii* that appear as shade trees in the Meadow Garden reappear here for structure in the open spaces between the raised beds. They are joined by mulberries, *Cornus tomentosa* and haskap (*Lonicera caerulea*), a shrubby fruiting honeysuckle which produces a tart but nutritious alternative to blueberries. The winters push the harsh weather into the Productive Gardens and, to date, the trees have borne the brunt of the snow drifts. Woody material is slow to establish in Hokkaido if it is not indigenous and, after ten years, the fruit trees that are tolerant are beginning to show their resistance. Those that are not, such as the Japanese apricot, *Prunus mume*, are falling by the wayside and illustrate the reality of trying to extend the boundaries of hardiness.

To the far side of the café, a greenhouse provides shelter for growing plants on and a nursery the space to produce plants for the garden. These areas are out of bounds to the public, but to the other side of the fence that screens this area are the Rose Garden, Orchard and trial beds. Every garden needs a place to experiment with new material, to test it for the climate and appropriateness for its setting, and we have an evolving collection of plants grown here from seed and cuttings, usually three of each plant, grown on for five years to observe them and test their suitability. Once tried and tested, plants are bulked up or planted directly into the Meadow Garden or the cutting areas.

Opposite: The garden is tended on principles of *satoyama*. All the staking materials and plant supports are harvested from the forest at the end of winter and early spring. Time is set aside to put care and thoughtfulness in each activity.

Overleaf: The cutting garden beds are informally planted with annuals and change every year. Dahlias, amaranthus and *Nicotiana mutabilis* combine with cosmos in this bed and provide flowers for the tables of the café.

1

2

1. A squash and pumpkin bed 2. An autumnal display of pumpkins including 'Rouge Vif d'Etampes', 'Turk's Turban' and 'Ebisu' 3. The Garden Café sits at the far end of the Meadow Garden 4. Raised beds allow a rotation of vegetables, herbs and flowers for cutting 5. The Kitchen Garden in high summer

Overleaf: After the first November snow the graphic simplicity of the Kitchen Garden layout is revealed from the veranda of the Garden Café.

3

4

5

The Orchard, where we are running a trial of cold-tolerant apple varieties, wraps around the Productive Gardens and marks the outer ripple of productivity. As the climate changes the apples may become more viable, but in the meantime they provide us with an interesting experiment. An area of soft fruit in the Orchard in turn wraps the Rose Garden and allows visitors an easy opportunity to forage as they loop their way back in to the cultivated grounds or decide to break out across the stream and out into the wider landscape of the Earth Garden.

The Rose Garden

The original Garden Masterplan included fields of the Apothecary's Rose, *Rosa gallica* var. *officinalis*, one of the oldest commercially productive roses, planted on an agricultural scale. These were intended to provide seasonal drama and the material to distil rose oil and its by-products for confectionery, food, cosmetics and perfumery. As the idea evolved, it became clear that it would be more interesting to broaden the story of the rose for visitors and to illustrate how it made its way into a more domestic world through selection and horticulture.

The Japanese interest in traditional Western-style gardens runs through the eight gardens on the Hokkaido Garden Path and so, to a degree, the decision to create a Rose Garden was also influenced by an understanding of the need to provide an area of interest for visitors at this end of the horticultural spectrum. Rose gardens represent the very opposite of naturalistic planting, so it was important to show the rose in a useful and productive light. With this in mind, and harking back to the original intent of the rose fields and the rose in production, we echoed the ordered layout of the Kitchen Garden for the most ornamental and highly bred plants and set them in a series of parallel raised oak beds. An informal arrangement beyond these includes a selection of roses that trace our relationship with the rose back in time to the pure species.

Old roses such as *Rosa damascena* and *Rosa gallica* var. *officinalis*, both of which have historically been harvested for their essential oils, illustrate our relationship with the rose as a crop plant. Indeed, they are harvested and made into cordial and ice cream in the Garden Café to demonstrate the fork-to-fork ethos of these gardens. Old roses that predate the introduction of the recurrent-flowering modern hybrids are included to illustrate the efforts made by breeders to refine a plant that became a symbol of the civilized world. The hardy *Rosa gallica* appears in selections such as the striped 'Rosa Mundi' and the deep purple 'Tuscany Superb'. Though they bloom just once in the year, these plants have stood the test of time.

We had already found through experimentation that the species roses were the most resilient this far north, but this is far from an absolute rule. *Rosa sericea* subsp. *omeiensis* f. *pteracantha* burned above the snow cover to the point of not being worth growing, while *Rosa moyesii* has taken four to five years to attain stature, but is now doing well. In the Meadow Garden *Rosa glauca*, by contrast, has proved not to need protection and

The wildest roses are planted informally on the margins of the Rose Garden, the most cultivated are reserved for the central raised beds. Here *Rosa macrophylla*, a once-blooming rose, goes on to form hips in the autumn.

1

2

3

1. The David Austin recurrent-flowering roses at the centre of the garden with the old-fashioned and species roses behind and the Meadow Garden beyond 2. *Rosa gallica* 'Tuscany Superb' (Gallica) 3. *Rosa spinosissima* 'Dunwich Rose' 4. *Rosa* 'The Lark Ascending' (David Austin)

4

5. The roses are picked daily and floated in water bowls in the plant laboratory 6. *Rosa* 'The Lady's Blush' 7. *Rosa spinosissima* and *Paeonia* 'Buckeye Belle' grouped around a seat that overlooks the garden

5

6

7

has survived above the snowline where it has been exposed to the chill of freezing winds. *Rosa spinosissima* is perfectly adapted to growing this far north without protection, while the eglantine, *Rosa rubiginosa* (syn. *R. eglanteria*), also from northern Europe, has not been hardy and our plan to use its apple-scented foliage by the paths has been thwarted.

Almost without exception, climbing roses have failed and we have decided it is not viable to take them from their supports and lay them beneath the snow for protection in the winter. This is common practice in the colder regions of North America, but requires energy not worth expending in Hokkaido where the autumn preparations are already busy enough ahead of winter.

In making our selections for the Rose Garden we worked closely with Michael Marriot, the rosarian at David Austin Roses. He has had extensive experience in the coldest states of the USA where rose culture is successful. There, the practice of 'winterizing' to ripen the wood by allowing the last flowers to form seed (rather than deadheading and then wrapping the plants for winter) allow the plants to survive sub-zero temperatures. More importantly, Michael had also been working on mainland Japan, a climate not without its problems due to the humidity. The cool summers in Hokkaido would prove to be ideal during the growing season, but the island would provide new challenges in winter.

When the Rose Garden was built, it was the first time the repeat-flowering David Austin roses had been planted extensively in the region. However, we were keen that they should be the centrepiece of the garden, since they represent the most up-to-date breeding for longevity and health, as well as for their relaxed mood that draws from the character of the Old Roses.

It was important that we worked within our limits, which were defined first by the climate and then by the amount of time it would take to protect any rose that needed help to get through the Hokkaido winter. It was also important that the roses could be maintained organically to be in tune with the overall ethos of the Millennium Forest. In terms of effort, and indeed the principle of 'cheating winter', it is questionable whether we should be putting the time and energy into roses that need such protection, but the pay off – the opulence of the more ornamental roses – rewards those visitors who need some coaxing to look more closely at the world through plants.

There were originally 50 varieties of David Austin roses in the collection that has been tested in the Hokkaido climate. The best and strongest have soon shown themselves and the range now totals around 40 with beds arranged by colour through reds, oranges and hot pinks fading to softer pinks to one side of the path and yellows, apricot and peach fading to white to the other. To keep the collection feeling connected to the wild, selections of single roses such as 'Morning Mist' and 'The Alexandra Rose' are included among the doubles, and semi-doubles such as 'The Lark Ascending' are used wherever possible to allow ease of pollination to insects, which cannot access the doubles.

Previous pages: Looking back towards the Garden Café. The Plant Laboratory, where displays from the garden are arranged daily, is beneath the pitched roof to the left.

Opposite, above: The David Austin roses are at the very limit of their hardiness in Hokkaido and need winter protection in October to protect them from freezing. *Below:* The Rose Garden in midwinter with the Orchard beyond and the mountains that bring the weather from the north.

Midori Shintani

From earth to table

The prime season for a particular ingredient is called *shun* in Japanese. We believe that the taste of *shun* is the most delicious of the year, and contains a lot of nutrients that we need at this point in the season. Eating seasonal ingredients deeply connects the biorhythm of humans to nature. *Shun* as well means the special seasonal appearance of plants such as cherry blossom and autumn leaves. *Shun* is the wisdom to lead a healthy life in harmony with nature. Welcoming *shun* unites people. Like many Japanese, I grew up sharing pleasures to celebrate *shun* with my family and friends.

I was a child who loved to help my mother in the kitchen. When plants in the mountains and fields started moving in spring, we picked young leaves of yomogi (*Artemisia indica* var. *maximowiczii*) from the riverbanks and made rice cakes with them together at home. They gave a vivid green colour to rice cakes, and we felt a breath of spring when their aroma filled the kitchen. Sometimes I was in charge of picking young leaves of sansho (*Zanthoxylum piperitum*) in the garden. We ground them to bring out the scent of the season, and ate freshly harvested bamboo shoots with sansho-flavoured miso.

When the harvest season of summer vegetables and fruits began we ate seasonal ingredients that contain a lot of water and vitamins in order to counteract the hot, humid summer. Wearing my *yukata* (casual summer kimono), eating a gigantic watermelon and watching fireworks was a favourite summer tradition. Crunchy whole cucumbers and tomatoes, homemade pickled aubergines and succulent peaches were also the taste of summer.

In the autumn, I climbed persimmon trees in my friend's garden and harvested baskets full of fruit. I hung them under the eaves of our house with my mother.

Midori in the Kitchen Garden.

Foraged shoots of Japanese butterbur, *Petasites japonica* subsp. *giganteus* (fuki).

At this time of the year, brownish-orange persimmons lined the eaves all over the countryside. With its melting flesh and condensed sweetness, a long-awaited *hoshigaki* (dried persimmon) was the best pleasure in winter.

We enjoy edible gardening with the concept of *shun* at the Tokachi Millennium Forest. Since most foods today are easily available throughout the year due to developments in greenhouse cultivation and distribution systems, we value the importance of knowing each season through the food of *shun*. The Garden Café is a place for our visitors to experience 'from earth to table' with our harvest from the forest, the Kitchen Garden, the Orchard and the Rose Garden. In sandwiches at the Garden Café, the fillings seasonally change following the harvest. One flavourful bite allows our visitors to realize what is growing in the garden now and they often get a delightful surprise from eating unknown edible plants.

When we hear the croaking of frogs spawning in the pond in April, we know that the forage season will shortly begin. At this moment I find young buds of fuki (*Petasites japonicus* subsp. *giganteus*) pushing their way up through the snow and my heart leaps with joy, as if thin ice cracks and melted snow flows out. We excitedly fly out of the greenhouse and harvest their buds in the field. The raw buds are bitter and must be processed quickly to mellow out their harshness, so staff of the Garden Café wait in front of a huge pot of boiling water in the kitchen for us to come back from foraging. We make fuki-miso (petasites miso paste) with cooked petasites, and this is the first flavour of the season for our visitors at the Millennium Forest. The bitterness of mountain vegetables wakes up our bodies which have been sleeping through the long winter and celebrates a new season coming.

Once the forest awakens, plants sprout one after another. Most mountain vegetables have a pleasant flavour in their young shoots, leaves or stems, so we spend every day foraging and harvesting edible plants such as *Allium victorialis* subsp. *platyphyllum*, *Matteuccia struthiopteris*, *Aralia cordata* and *Reynoutria japonica* (syn. *Fallopia japonica*). Harvesting delicious and invasive plants can also be a way of thinning them out to have a thoughtful balance of the vegetation on the forest floor.

At the beginning of July, when the last snow of the Hidaka Mountains disappears, the Rose Garden attracts us with the magnificent fragrance of the English and Old Roses. The Garden Café takes on a festive mood for the first flush, and we immediately shift the decoration of cakes from cherry and magnolia to rose. Rose petals also appear on the fresh green salad harvested from the Kitchen Garden. Garnished with other edible flowers and herbs, it looks like a garden on the plate. We also carefully preserve the rich fragrance of roses in a syrup to enjoy for the rest of the summer.

Choosing the right varieties is one of the most important keys to our organic gardening. Every summer we do a trial of varieties of specific crops to find good varieties to select as Millennium Forest standards, such as Hokkaido's abundant potato varieties, heirloom tomatoes, local bean varieties, beets, lettuces, squash, blueberry and rose, as well as scabious, dahlia and cosmos as cut flowers for the table. We collect samples and study the production characteristics, physical characteristics and culinary or arrangement characteristics of each variety. Sometimes our student gardeners bravely submit to blind taste tests, at which we always end up laughing. I like to see everyone looking so serious to discover a new flavour, and then looking so happy for the pure joy that tasting this new food brought them.

Every year the garden team
undertakes taste trials of new varieties.
Here, blueberries.

THE MEADOW GARDEN

Naturalism in the Japanese garden

Naturalistic planting in Japanese horticulture was still in its infancy when we were planning the Garden Masterplan, and the 0.8-hectare (2-acre) site for the Meadow Garden provided us with an opportunity to make a grand gesture – one that was appropriate to our ethos of working closely with nature and using the environment as a guide and inspiration. Where the light-touch management in the Entrance Garden might be lost to the casual visitor, a new and experimental garden would help to draw the world of plants into new focus. The Meadow Garden would feel comfortable for its easy pathways and places of contemplation. It would feel familiar for referencing the Japanese tradition of *shakkei*, with the borrowed view of the mountains made intimate and reframed by the planting. It would also be a place that would appear to be completely in context as the visitor emerged from the shadows of trees, crossed the stream and broke out into the light to find a planting of subtly heightened intensity.

Previously a paddock, the site is framed on the lower side by a brutal cut made earlier to clear the grazing alongside the Entrance Forest, while to the upper side are the Hidaka Mountains and open landscape. The far side is contained by the Goat Farm buildings and the road, while a fast-running stream separates the area from the Earth Garden.

The first moves in the design process were to bridge the stream with a crossing that fixed an axis starting at the Kisara Building that sits on the edge of the Earth Garden. A slight incline beside the stream towards the mountain was enhanced with three levels that step the garden up from the forest edge. The first is the meridian boardwalk through the centre of the site, the second a contour that reaches the higher ground made from an extended limb of the Earth Garden. The level changes serve to make the space feel more dynamic and help to define a series of places that each have their own habitat: a damp woodland clearing on the lower level, an open mid-level meadow along the meridian and a high meadow that rises with the landform and has the mountain view as its backdrop.

An embracing bund which holds the upper part of the garden was planted with shrubs to enhance its presence while still maintaining a visual connection to the mountain. These woody plants continue along the stream edge with willow and alder to screen the garden from the mountain winds and provide a compression point as one crosses the bridge. Birch, oak and magnolias continue back along the woodland to fray the clean cut where woodland previously met pasture and create dappled light for the lower levels.

The built form of the Meadow Garden is kept deliberately light so that the paths and changes of level are integrated and help to step the garden away from the woodland and upward toward the mountain. The central boardwalk, which was inspired by the

Opposite: In the upper reaches of the Meadow Garden, the variegated form of *Miscanthus sinensis* (susuki), *M. s. 'Zebrinus'*, marks the season with late flower and makes a link to the landscape that lies beyond.

Overleaf: The crossing into the Meadow Garden bridges the fast-moving stream alongside the Earth Garden and runs directly into the central axis of the boardwalk. Native willows, which were introduced on the stream banks, form a natural arch and shelter the planting from the prevailing winds that come down from the mountains.

1

2

3

4

wide, braided rivers that scour Hokkaido with snowmelt water, runs through the middle of the site to connect the Earth Garden with the Farm Garden and its associated buildings. The boardwalk is made from larch sleepers harvested from the plantations that are slowly being removed from the forest. As it sweeps through the garden the wide walkway separates the lower damp meadows from the mid-level openness that welcomes you as you enter from the bridge. The boardwalk is cantilevered on the lower side to enhance the feeling of being above damp ground and meets the ground on the level to the other side. Secondary paths which step down and away from the main path are deliberately narrowed so that they feel like animal tracks weaving through the planting. You walk on these in single file. On the upper levels, the narrowed paths run along the top side of a corten steel terraced wall that separates the central sections of the garden from the upper meadows.

Though the frayed edges of the garden are deliberately dappled to make the link with the surrounding woodland, the general openness of the Meadow Garden provides a valuable new environment for plants. The light conditions support a different range of plants from those that grow in the woodland and allow us to extend the season beyond the natural peak of high summer when the forest closes over and the woodland plants have climaxed. The new palette draws Japanese natives together with overseas introductions so that the juxtaposition of the two reframes the natives alongside their garden companions.

The principles of the planting

While I draw upon the existing environment as inspiration and the essence of a place drives my decision-making in the design process, understanding how plants coexist in their setting is key. Making a naturalistic garden means not only looking at the individuals but at the communities of plants and how they perform as one, so it was only fitting to emulate the richness of the forest floor in the new garden. This addition to the park would take the gentle husbandry practised in the Entrance Forest one step further to illustrate how applied horticulture can be used to create an enhanced and modified environment which is adapted closely to its setting.

The planting in the Meadow Garden is designed to work as one entity so that it evolves in much the same way as its namesake. In a meadow the plants have evolved to coexist, species occupying their windows of flowering over the season, one eclipsing the next from spring to autumn. The first are happy to drop into the shadows in the wake of their successors and the later-flowering plants have the reserves to push through the early risers. In the course of a growing season, there will be an almost unbroken opportunity for pollination and interest for wildlife as plants come to seed.

Though highly competitive, each species has found its niche both above and below ground. The place where a damp seam runs encourages the moisture-lovers, whereas a shadowy area will naturally be colonized by those plants that have evolved in those

1. Construction of the Meadow Garden and adjoining Kitchen Garden in 2006, with the central boardwalk almost complete. The setts that form the hard standing in the foreground are widely spaced to be inter-sown with grass to soften this area. 2. Each mix was trialled within its allocated area in a 3 x 3m (10 x 10ft) grid to give one winter and a growing season to test viability and the composition of the matrix. 3. The Meadow Garden immediately after planting in 2008. 4. Looking back towards the entrance bridge in 2018 with the woodland wrap now grown and the tiers that run through the garden clearly visible.

Overleaf: The Meadow Garden in early summer with the buffer of the woodland wrap now sheltering it from the open ground which lies beyond.

conditions. A meadow is a highly dynamic environment, stable for periods of cultural evenness, but reactive should conditions change suddenly due to flood, drought or fire. The most stable meadows are those controlled by managed grassland for hay and grazing. The best are sometimes hundreds of years old and represent a close evolution and synergy between humans and nature.

To emulate the complexity of the meadow and its natural order, I developed a series of plant mixes as the first step in the process. The combinations within the mixes would echo the rhythms of a meadow as it rises from dormancy in the spring and then changes as one species supersedes the next throughout the season. The succession within the plant community ensures it is dynamic and engaging until it runs to seed in the autumn.

In terms of providing a manageable order, the mixes allow us to choose groups of plants that are happy in each other's company and complementary in terms of providing contrast and seasonal interest. Though the zoning is not obvious when looking at the garden initially, the mixes allow for changes across the site that can adapt to the differing conditions, be it the shady woodland edge or the high open ground in full light. The mixes also provide shifts in mood, with some being more complex and engaging close to the main boardwalk and others allowing for an easy flow so that the eye can travel.

The matrix

I wanted the garden to have the quality of a natural environment, as though the plants had chosen their own place. The mixes provided the raw ingredients which were then combined in a deliberately random matrix. The aim was to let the plants achieve their own equilibrium so that once the anchor plants – trees, shrubs and key perennials – were put in place, the matrix would run between them like river water around boulders. As the areas were large enough, I hoped that the different species would assert themselves where they found a niche that favoured their needs.

Having started with 17, there are now 19 distinct mixes reflecting changes that have happened in the last decade. Each is carefully calibrated by percentage. When the planting was first designed, there were on average five to eight plants in each mix. Each contained a small percentage of emergent plants to give height and stand proud of their companions and a similar number of feature plants such as *Baptisia*, *Paeonia* or *Rodgersia* to provide a mid-level anchor and textural character. The remaining 70–80 per cent were lower-level perennials that would mingle to cover the ground.

This layering in the planting was designed into the mixes to ensure that there would be seasonal change as one layer rose up to eclipse the next. Compatibility was key, the lower perennials being happy to sit in the shadow of the mixes where there were taller species. The layering would also provide succession of interest throughout the season and the opportunity of planting with textural interest and colour change.

In order to replicate the apparent disorganization of nature I needed to create a system that would simulate randomness when the garden was set out from plan.

Overleaf: Mix J in mid-season. Emergents Veronicastrum sibiricum subsp. yezoense, Vernonia fasciculata, Vernonia arkansana 'Mammuth' and Sanguisorba 'Cangshan Cranberry' rise up to leave the minglers behind. Baptisia australis forms a mid-layer component.

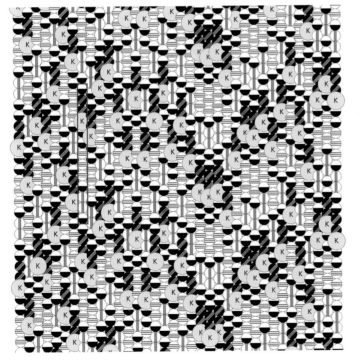

Mix D1

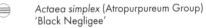 *Actaea simplex* (Atropurpureum Group) 'Black Negligee'

 *Galium odoratum*

 *Geranium phaeum* var. *phaeum* 'Samobor'

Ⓚ *Kirengeshoma palmata*

◑ *Polygonatum odoratum*

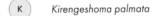

Above: Mix D1, grown in and forming a close community after establishment. *Left:* The plans for the D1 mix illustrating the random layout including the components of the mix and the strand of 'DNA' which, when randomly repeated, simulates the natural communities of plants that are found in a meadow.

First we created a linear unit, like a strand of DNA or a musical refrain, that contained all of the plants in each mix in their percentage combinations. The strands were laid next to each other in rows, but in each row the strand started at a different point so that each row would never have the strand repeat identically. It was important when we designed the mixes that the emergent plants that provided accent and the key character plants that would offer stability were few enough within the mix for there to be space for the mingled plants among them. There would need to be enough of the lower-level minglers to move between them to provide the cohesion and the layering that I had been closely observing over the course of the growing season on the forest floor, with several plants occupying the same space and adapting to each other's company.

It was a new system and one that I knew would need an informed eye on the ground to make the necessary adjustments, but in order to communicate this new approach across culture and language barriers it was important to build a system into the design from the beginning. Once the garden was up and running the system would then be managed responsively by the gardeners.

Elements to modulate the matrix

Towards the boundaries on the lower levels, woody plants feather the garden into the forest and provide a gathering shade to walk through. Though native, *Cercidiphyllum japonicum* and *Stewartia japonica* are at the limit of their hardiness here. They intensify the woodland edge in terms of variation, while *Aralia elata*, lifted from the forest, covers for their slow period of establishment with rapid growth and a ranging habit. The deep shrubberies that wrap the garden are simply mulched and deliberately not underplanted so that they provide a buffer to the plants that we have introduced, which we do not want escaping into the wider environment.

Emerging shrubs such as *Rosa glauca* and amelanchier and impressive perennials such as *Persicaria alpina* that have volume act as interlopers and help to punctuate the matrix, providing resting points for the eye. The large perennials are used much like the shrubs, with mother colonies giving way to outliers which jump from mix to mix much as you would see in an evolving community in the wild. The volumes break an expanse of one mix and then allow it to continue uninterrupted so that the rhythm in the garden changes as you make your passage along the pathways. The volumes also act to frame and reframe smaller views within the garden, so that you are encouraged to look from the macro to the micro and back again.

Another key element is the hedges of *Calamagrostis* × *acutiflora* 'Karl Foerster' that sweep through the garden in large brushstrokes. They serve as a bold and graphic counterpoint to the detail in the matrix and connect visually to the grasslands of the mountain foothills. Moving as one entity throughout the garden, they harness the wind or give resonance to stillness. Importantly, once they are grown to full height they act as scene-changers between the mixes and the colour fields when the garden is flowering.

Opposite: Native Aralia elata is used as a woody emergent in Mix D1. In the background, Rosa glauca provides constancy and volume against the froth of Gillenia trifoliata in full flower early in the season.

Overleaf: Persicaria amplexicaulis 'Atrosanguinea' provides a peak of high summer colour in the centre of the garden.

Colour is a significant protagonist in the garden and provides an immediate means of changing the mood throughout the seasons and from area to area. The colour emerges *en masse* as one species climaxes in a mix and is then replaced by another. At peak points these waves overlap for vibrancy and there are a number of contrasting colour fields throughout the garden which are designed to change the quality of each space. The strongest colours are physically divided by the formal swathes of calamagrostis, which filter the opposing colours and act as palate cleansers.

At the edge of the woodland the colour is calm, weighted by green, plum tones, pale lemon yellow and blues which are most visible in the dappled light. A reliance on white throughout the mixes here provides levity and gives some sparkle on dull days. Above the meridian pathway, and close to it on the lower levels, the colour becomes more saturated, with less green and more reliance on flower. Mauves, dusky pink and the lightness of *Gillenia trifoliata* start the season here, later replaced by blues, violet and the dusky red of *Persicaria amplexicaulis* 'Atrosanguinea'. The peak point of strongest colour is underpinned by a consistent low-level cloud of creamy *Eurybia divaricata* and mauve *Origanum laevigatum*. Here in the heart of the garden the rich colours are designed to hold your attention.

Initially concealed from the central pathway by the volume of a number of *Rosa glauca* and charging the upper meadow where there is a step change in level is an area that is energized by red. *Euphorbia griffithii* 'Fireglow' and *Sanguisorba officinalis* 'Red Thunder' provide the foundation of heat and an invigorating atmosphere. Beyond, and partially concealed by a veil of a calamagrostis, the red colour field gives way to yellow. Hidden by the veil of grasses until you are led there by the intimate path system, this area is a complete immersion. Bright against the dark pine boundary, it is designed to flare in full sun and provide energy as you exit the garden.

Seasonal variation is central to the planting and the garden changes dramatically from week to week as the matrix allows for the big gesture of one plant to come into its own *en masse*. This affects the physical reach of colour appearing and disappearing in the garden which, from one week to the next, can radically alter the composition. As autumn comes and the asters dim, a new palette of autumnal tones is infused into the planting to make the link with the forest. In late September brown, black, sepia, bone and earth tones replace a garden that was, just weeks before, vibrant with flower.

Seasonal flux also influences the height and relationship between plants as the planting evolves over the growing season. The rhythms echo the dramatic shifts seen in a real meadow, with one species performing for a week at its peak and then dimming as another takes over. Early in the season your eye can travel from boundary to boundary in the Meadow Garden as the first stirrings appear at ground level. As the season gathers pace, the early emergents rise to provide differentiation to the horizontal and the calamagrostis hedges provide division. The layering continues to alter the scale and experience of the garden as it fills and reaches its peak in late August. September sees it falling away gently, with transparency reappearing again as autumn has its influence.

Opposite, above: Warm colour in Mix K at the heart of the garden with *Eupatorium maculatum* Atropurpureum Group emerging through *Persicaria amplexicaulis* 'Atrosanguinea'. *Below:* A river of *Achillea* 'Coronation Gold' passes through the yellow matrix of Mix C. *Coreopsis verticillata* 'Zagreb' provides the first wave of intense colour in late July, joined and then eclipsed by *Rudbeckia fulgida* var. *sullivantii* 'Goldsturm'.

THE MEADOW PLANTS

Reframing the native plants

The richness of the forest floor on Hokkaido is almost overwhelming when you encounter it for the first time. Plants that you have treasured as 'exotics' back in the West grow wild there in the way they were meant to – not as solitary specimens, but happily in company. Arisaema and anemone, palest pink meadowsweet and the finest thalictrum; hostas standing tall and muscling for their position and lofty daylilies hovering on wiry stems in the shadows.

Although, as a Westerner, it is unlikely that I will ever take this floral diversity for granted, I wanted to make sure that the familiarity of the local vegetation was also thrown into a new light for Japanese visitors. The Meadow Garden was to provide this opportunity. By juxtaposing the best of the native plant material with plants selected in the West for their gardenworthiness I hoped to reframe the native plants. The wild hostas would sit alongside new partners to show them to best advantage and the hemerocallis that had nodded quietly in the Entrance Forest would reappear centre-stage in the new light of a garden setting.

When selecting non-natives, we looked to areas of the world that share a similar hardiness rating to Hokkaido's Zone 4, which is equivalent to USDA Zone 5 and equates to an average minimum winter temperature of -29 to -23°C (-20 to -10°F). Areas of Northern Europe, Eurasia and Northern America provide similar conditions, with four distinct seasons and an extended period of winter dormancy. We were also careful to choose plants that were not known to be invasive and had a proven track record in terms of garden performance. The majority were selected for long-term stability with the aim of building reliable and long-lived partnerships between plants to once again emulate the systems in the plant communities that have evolved over decades on the forest floor. Short-lived self-seeding perennials such as *Knautia macedonica* were included for their pioneering habits and ability to respond quickly to change.

In terms of ethos and aesthetics, it was important that all the plants we introduced were in the spirit of the vegetation that already existed on site. Everything was selected to have a natural appearance that would not look out of place alongside the natives. The choices were limited to either straight species or named forms that were close to the species. Flowers remained small or uncomplicated, with no doubles that felt highly bred or made pollination difficult. The planting was carefully selected so that it was tonally right, taking the lead from the foliage shapes and colouration of plants in the forest and often looking to equivalent plants that occur both in Japan and North America. Though I was deliberately heightening the intensity of the aesthetic in the

In Mix F, native
Hydrangea paniculata,
Filipendula camschatica and
Lilium auratum are combined
with introduced *Persicaria*
amplexicaulis 'Alba',
Phlox paniculata 'David'
and *Astrantia major*
subsp. *involucrata*.

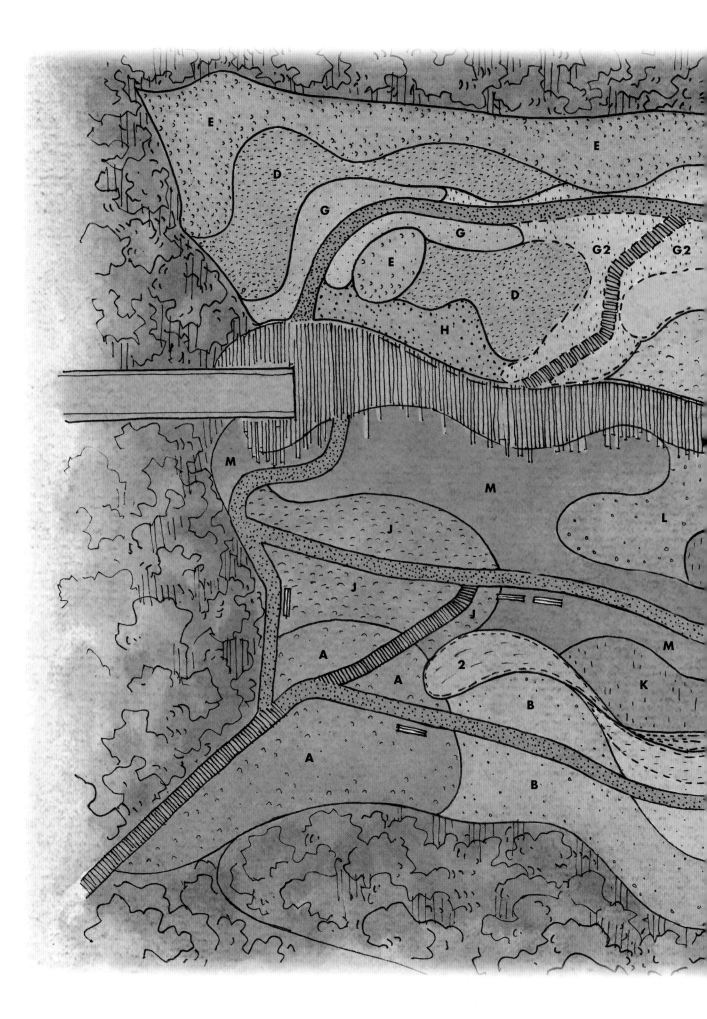

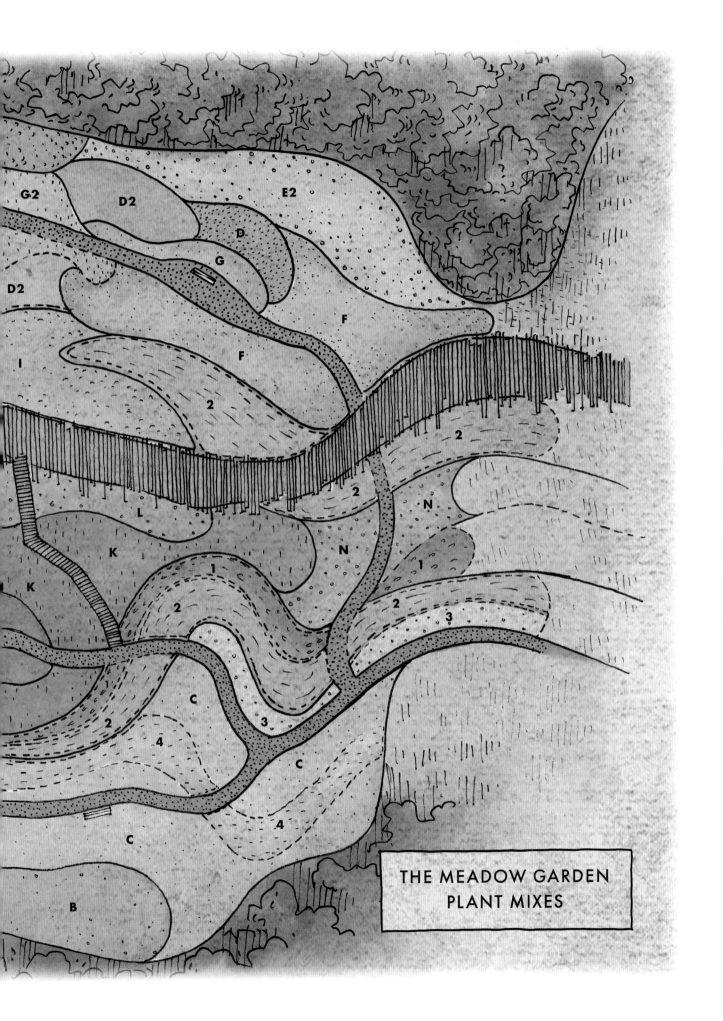

THE MEADOW GARDEN
PLANT MIXES

Meadow Garden, I wanted the plants from overseas to feel as if they were meant to be in each other's company when combined with the Japanese natives.

Mr Omori, of the coastal Omori Garden in Hiroo, was a pioneer nurseryman on the island who made it possible to source the plant material we needed in Hokkaido. Through working closely together, we began to identify a palette of plants that would grow in this extreme climate. At the time he was the only nurseryman on Hokkaido who was trading in perennials. He had already trialled a wide variety of plants from overseas by importing from the USA but, more importantly, he was open to expanding his palette and raising stock in the numbers we needed. The initial planting in 2008 required 35,000 perennials, but a year in advance we planted a 3 x 3m (10 x 10ft) trial area of each of the 17 mixes to test hardiness and the principles of the planting matrix.

We made minor adjustments, swapping a less hardy miscanthus from Honshu for one that was more suitable to Hokkaido and simplifying the calamagrostis hedges when I saw how well the plants had sailed through the first winter. In the original plans they were combined in places with a matching band of *Helianthus salicifolius*. These were good moves, made with time on our side, and they gave us confidence in our plans.

Steering the plant mixes

The garden was planted, as planned, in the spring of 2008, so one of my key tasks when I first met Midori was to explain that the garden was intended to be an echo of a natural environment. We walked into the forest and looked at the natural plant associations, the succession and the layering from the ground up to the tallest emergents. It was summer and already the first layers of trillium and anemone were going into dormancy beneath the mid-storey plants. Carex and filipendula were filling out to cover for the first ephemerals and rising up tall were stands of cardiocrinum and angelica. We discussed the importance of the Entrance Forest and the Meadow Garden being in easy dialogue and the influence of the native plant communities upon the workings and the aesthetic of the Meadow Garden.

We also touched on the realities of maintaining something that was designed to evolve and would not, by definition, be something we could entirely plan for. Our yearly meetings and email communications help in steering the direction and we have responded to the planting as gardeners, since we are not ecologists, but always with an eye to letting the planting lead the way. Of course, there have been challenges, because in truth the complexity of a real meadow is far more dynamic. Just 1 sq m (11sq ft) might contain 20–30 species and the competitive nature of the ecosystem is consequently self-monitoring. I had hoped that we would be able to strike a balance in the matrix but, to illustrate the point, the following spring Midori sent me an image of the *Thermopsis lupinoides* from Mix B, which had run riot and was clearly bent on total domination. I had seen this plant in the wild in Japan, but had not tried and tested it *in situ* for more than a year in our test beds. It was also a plant I had used in the UK, but without the competition provided by a natural ecosystem, or indeed the adaptive natives that it has evolved with, it had seized the window of opportunity and taken off. Midori had carefully lifted an entire plant which was laid out like a botanical specimen. The root spread must have been all of 2m (6 1/2ft) across and it was good to know the garden would be in safe hands given Midori's attention to detail and horticultural rigour. Each scrap of root was painstakingly removed and the crisis averted.

We do have other Japanese natives such as *Lysimachia clethroides*, *Hakonechloa macra* and *Houttuynia cordata* that have also proved to be invasive in the setting of the garden, but not to such a degree as the fateful thermopsis. In some cases this has meant losing the detail of less competitive plants in the mix and letting the dominant components tough it out with those plants that are up to the challenge. We have had to choose where to fight the battles.

As the garden has evolved in its first ten years, we have been able to see what is working and what is struggling. Having reached a point where the original mixes had generally achieved an equilibrium, we have since been adjusting and augmenting the plantings to make them work harder. The initial principles have remained in place, but the matrix has required manipulation. Sometimes a mix has needed a percentage reduction of a plant that has become too dominant, such as the *Filipendula camschatica*, but there have also been unexpected failures. With the exception of the thermopsis, we have given all plants a minimum of three, usually five, years to confirm that they are not suited to the climate and explore potential replacements. *Levisticum officinale* and *Ligularia* 'The Rocket', for instance, have simply not thrived. We also thought that *Asclepias incarnata* from the American prairies would have found a parallel climate, but it too has merely limped on.

The mixes respond differently from year to year to climatic changes that favour or discourage a particular species. Natural life cycles also assert their peaks and troughs and our annual walks in the garden help us to decide how to steer the garden in the comings year. The climate also encourages a fast turnaround. Plants such as *Salvia nemorosa* 'Caradonna', though perfectly hardy, need adding to every year since their natural life cycle on Hokkaido is around three years rather than the five we can expect in the UK before they need replacement or division. The short-lived plants such as *Knautia macedonica* are treated like biennials and allowed to seed into gaps, with the oldest plants removed as they start to splay. They are worth this effort for their summer-long display of flower. A small number of *Echinacea* 'Hot Summer' have also been added to add drama as you enter the garden from the bridge. Though the red echinaceas tend not to be reliable perennials, they prove their worth with ornamental impact, and so are replaced year on year. Such additions to the mixes and responsiveness to the ebb and flow keep the mixes feeling vital and yearly change prevents the garden from ever feeling static. In maintaining a garden of this size with a limited workforce we have to measure the energies that are available and our yearly plans forecast tasks that need to be carried out the following year. The first five years were about getting to know how this new

Overleaf: Late August, looking through Mix M with Agastache nepetoides and Panicum virgatum 'Heavy Metal' emerging in the foreground. Running away into the distance with Eurybia × herveyi, is Mix L.

environment was reacting. We looked closely into hardiness and vigour and how the plants were adapting to living in such close company. The pioneers in the mixes soon asserted themselves, but waned as the slower-growing perennials gained their foothold. It was a process of observation and acting fast where imbalance was evident, but trying not to tamper where we saw the potential of a mix reaching equilibrium.

At five years, and once the woody plants were established in the mixes, we began to notice that certain perennials were losing their grip in the matrix, as a result of diminished vigour, and needed division. The calamagrostis hedges have been split over three years, because it would simply be too much to do in one spring and we now plan on repeating this on a five-year cycle. Each plant has its own life span in the mixes and the long-lived plants such as the baptisia are proving their worth for being steadfast. We aspire to longevity, but even the plants that stay put and do well need adjusting as they shift the balance by becoming too dominant. The art is in knowing where to adjust and where not to and then responding in timely fashion to maintain the balance, both in the community of plants and in the aesthetic which, by definition, is subject to change as the garden matures.

The perennial planting is divided into three main areas that each has a distinct mood designed to modulate the atmospheres in the Meadow Garden. They change gently from the intimacy and shelter of the woodland wrap on the lower levels below the main path, out into the open of the centre of the garden and then up onto the higher ground where the climate is directly influenced by the air from the mountains. The following overviews of the planting in each of these areas looks at the mechanics of how the mixes have worked as individual communities and also how they combine as a whole to modulate the garden as you move through it. The complete plant mix lists are on pages 274-7.

The woodland wrap and planted buffer

I wanted to wrap the Meadow Garden with a woody planting that would separate it physically from the forest and provide shelter between the openness of the Earth Garden and the retained views to the backdrop of the mountains. These buffers are mulched and without groundcovers so that we are able to monitor any self-seeding and prevent the cultivated garden from having any influence over the wild ground beyond it.

The bunded landform that extends from the Earth Garden and holds the Meadow Garden on its open side works on the principle of *shakkei,* the capturing of a borrowed view. The planted rise separates the Meadow Garden from the Rose Garden immediately beyond it, while making a strong and certain link to the mountains beyond. Their proximity is foreshortened with a careful choice of plant material, which plays with scale and diminishes the feeling of distance. The shrubby *Pinus mugo* echoes a much larger tree in its form and plays a key role by connecting directly to the larch and the oaks on the foothills. This shrubby pine is maintained at no more than shoulder height so that the mountains are never shielded.

The darkness and constancy of the pines is important to the garden and their stillness makes for a reliable evergreen backdrop in the immediate foreground. *Sorbaria sorbifolia*, a shrubby species from China which does not grow more than 1.5m (5 ft) in Hokkaido, is worked in among the pines to provide seasonal flux. The fine foliage of both plants allows the eye to travel rather than alight on the boundary planting, while the deciduous change and froth of the sorbaria's creamy flower echoes the shifts in the distant woodland.

The mountains are framed to either side of the view by *Salix alba* var. *sericea* (syn. *S. alba* f. *argentea*) to anchor the buildings of the Productive Gardens. These silvery willows rise out of the dark pines and provide a shimmer and contrast to the stillness at their feet. Their movement in the wind takes the eye up and out of the Meadow Garden and acts as a framing device with Japanese *Sorbus commixta* and native wild willows that have been planted along the stream edge to the opposite end of the bund. By framing the mountains to either side of the planted mound they are distilled and made part of the Meadow Garden.

Running along the garden side of the stream that separates this area from the openness of the Earth Garden is a protective wrap of willows that take the brunt of the weather. Hardwood cuttings were harvested from local colonies at the outset of the project and inserted directly into the banks. Chosen for their reliable speed, they are now pollarded on a rotation of three to five years so that the windbreak is never completely broken. They are encouraged to arch over the bridge that makes its way across the stream and also compress the entrance to the Meadow Garden so that you are aware of the stream beneath you before punching out into light and openness.

The woodland wrap continues along the forested boundary to the lower side of the garden where the original cut was made to clear the paddocks alongside the woodland. Fast-growing *Betula platyphylla* were mingled with slower-growing local oaks, *Quercus mongolica* subsp. *crispula*, and *Magnolia obovata* to make immediate links to the native woodland. Evergreens are almost absent from the native flora so a shrubby shy-flowering rhododendron was included to provide a lower-growing evergreen which works at a human scale to add density and provide a dark backdrop at eye level. *Magnolia kobus* and *Hydrangea paniculata* at the edge of the woodland buffer form a flowering edge where the woodland steps into the Meadow Garden. The magnolias are probably borderline hardy here and flower and leaf together in the late, fast spring, but the hydrangea is perfectly adapted to the conditions and contributes summer flower and a good physical presence.

The woodland glade

This area is made up of the mixes that sit at the woodland edge and feather into it to provide a continuity into shadow. They are designed to take both sun and dappled light and they run out into more open ground on the lower levels below the path. They have been chosen specifically for the lower ground which lies damp below the main path.

1. Mix D1 in May 2. *Iris × robusta* 'Gerald Darby' 3. *Aralia elata* step through an underplanting of *Geranium phaeum* var. *phaeum* 'Samobor' and *Polygonatum odoratum* 4. *Rosa sericea* subsp. *omeiensis* f. *pteracantha* 5. Spent flowers of *Actaea simplex* (Atropurpurea Group) 'Black Negligee' with *Symphyotrichum turbinellum*

2

Mixes D1 and D2

Mixes D1 and D2 sit on the edge of the woodland wrap and mark the transitions from wild to cultivated and from shade to light. The mixes were originally split over five areas and across two paths to provide continuity at this end of the woodland glade. There are common elements that run through both mixes, but there are differences between mixes D1 and D2 which reflect subtle variations in areas of light and shadow. As the shade trees have established microclimates, each of the areas has required alteration to respond to the evolving conditions and we now relate to Mix D being specific to each area. Two groups of trees step the woodland into the garden to form a glade. *Cercidiphyllum japonicum* and *Aralia elata* rise up to dapple Mix D1 and *Stewartia pseudocamellia* and a repeat of *Aralia elata* make the connection over the path into D2. *Rosa sericea* subsp. *omeiensis* f. *pteracantha* layer shadow into the most open areas and *Persicaria alpina* provides summer shade for lower-growing plants in the matrix. *Continued on page 184.*

Continued on page 184.

3

4

5

As you enter the Meadow Garden across the bridge you can step down into Mix D from the main central path onto a lower walk which is designed to capture an intimate mood and a glade-like atmosphere. Emergent trees and shrubs break away from the density of the adjoining woodland wrap to form a dappled area through which the paths meander. *Cercidiphyllum japonicum* (katsura), which occurs naturally on the main island of Honshu, has shown itself to be at the very edge of its hardiness on Hokkaido. As the shelter provided by the woodland wrap that forms the boundary on the lower levels has grown up, the katsura that come under its influence have begun to make extension growth. However, those out in the open are taking time, with winter damage sometimes outstripping the gain of summer growth. They have regrown as multi-stemmed shrubs, which still provide mid-storey benefit, and they may well become more tree-like in time.

The katsura grow out into Mix D, which over time we have adapted to cope with the evolving shade. In the damp conditions of Hokkaido the katsura foliage emits its distinctive smell of burnt sugar not just in the autumn but throughout the summer, so that you pass through the stillness here accompanied by perfume. The emerging foliage is copper before becoming emerald green. The simplicity of the leaf is good with everything and although the fast Hokkaido autumn sees it flare just briefly, the buttery colouring and perfume is good with the asters.

Further west in Sapporo *Stewartia pseudocamellia* thrive unhindered by winter, but here they too have succumbed to the wind chill from the Hidaka mountains. Over ten years, though, it can be seen that they are forming a community and a local microclimate that provides protection. It has been worth testing their hardiness as they complement the indigenous woodland and heighten the mood. The stewartias add sparkle with their simple summer flower and they colour well at the end of the season, turning copper at the same time as the wind anemones are flowering. Their mottled bark is notable when in its deciduous state and they make good company for the understorey matrix of perennials by not being competitive of root.

Magnolia denudata and *Rosa sericea* subsp. *omeiensis* f. *pteracantha*, which were both originally used in the glade as mid-storey shrubs, have both failed due to winter damage and, despite the presence of an endemic *Sambucus* (*racemosa* subsp. *kamtschatica*) the winters have also been too severe for *Sambucus nigra* 'Black Lace'. To add a mid-layer woody presence in this area, *Aralia elata* was moved from the forest and has been fast to establish and provide height without being dominant. This is important for the success of the perennial understorey. In the shadier parts we have also introduced *Hydrangea serrata* var. *megacarpa* from Hokkaido collections. Though it has been worthwhile testing the hardiness of plants brought to the Tokachi climate, the local plants can generally be relied upon to perform and cover for those that take more time to find their niche in the mixes.

The mixes flow in and out of the dappled areas with the shade-lovers demonstrating their favoured positions as they would in the forest. Sometimes this is very localized, for example a single *Kirengeshoma palmata* in Mix D1 preferring just the right amount of shelter and the local microclimate of shade close by. Likewise, the *Geranium phaeum* var. *phaeum* 'Samobor' and *Actaea simplex* (Atropurpurea Group) 'Black Negligee' favour the cooler places and burn in the sun. We have adapted to what the conditions tell us and allowed the matrix to evolve. Where an absence has become apparent in a mix – the early-flowering *Geranium phaeum* var. *phaeum* 'Samobor' and the late-to-flower *Actaea* not favouring the open areas, for instance – we adjust accordingly by making an addition to replace them. New plants that prefer the sun such as *Iris* × *robusta* 'Gerald Darby' and *Symphyotrichum turbinellum* fill the niche in the mix so that there is still a seasonal succession in the layering.

Close to the edge of the main path where it cantilevers to enhance the impression that the woodland glade is a lower, damper situation, hostas and native *Iris sanguinea* make an appearance in Mix I and link to the damp woodland of the Entrance Forest. Where trees give way to sunshine and the shade-tolerant matrix needs to adapt to more light, a stand of *Persicaria alpina* provides a continuity of scale to the shrubs. Their volume also gives additional shelter to the plants in the mixes that inhabit the woodland edge. The first flurry of spring ephemerals such as the trilliums and maianthemums are planted in their shadow and cover for them while the later growth of the persicaria is still young. When they are fully grown they provide their own cooling effect and sheltered microclimate for neighbouring perennials.

Hakonechloa macra from Honshu is happy on Hokkaido, but has done too well in Mix G; the pulmonaria and *Helleborus orientalis* that were designed to dip into its summer shade have been largely outcompeted. We tried various techniques of curbing the hakonechloa – an early summer cut and localized thinning – but in time we have accepted that it is only the strongest plants that can cohabit with this grass. The mix has been simplified and we use the hakonechloa as a consistent member of the matrix here to pull areas together and provide a cool, calm backdrop to more complex combinations nearby. It is important when you are walking through the garden that the small paths feel as if they are moving through one environment and the hakonechloa is a good example of a plant that jumps the paths to provide cohesion. Bold groups of plants are also used to draw the eye and *Symphyotrichum turbinellum* runs through several mixes to light up the lower sections of the garden in the autumn.

As the woodland glade comes into sunshine on the lower levels and transitions into Mix F, *Filipendula camschatica* forms a large stand that is shelter for the plants that live among it. This giant meadowsweet will grow to nearly 3m (10ft) in the nearby woodland, but out in the light it is more compact though reliably clump-forming. We have had to reduce the percentage of it in the mix several times to make room for a matrix of cool-growing *Astrantia major* subsp. *involucrata*, *Anemone sylvestris* 'Madonna' and *Lilium auratum* which flows among the meadowsweet and takes advantage of the localized microclimate they create. *Phlox paniculata* 'David' was introduced to provide an alternative volume when the balance of filipendula in the mix was recalibrated. *Angelica gigas* has finally begun to self-seed and echoes the *Angelica edulis* in the forest.

Overleaf: Trillium camschatcense and Galium odoratum perform early and then take shelter under Rodgersia podophylla on the edges of the woodland wrap in Mix E1.

1

Mixed D1 and D2 (continued from page 178)

Until the shade was established *Actaea simplex* (Atropurpurea Group) 'Black Negligee' and *Kirengeshoma palmata* proved sun-intolerant and have naturally retreated to the shadows. *Iris × robusta* 'Gerald Darby' replaced them as emergent verticals and *Symphyotrichum turbinellum* is a late-season emergent to run between the D mixes in the open areas. *Galium odoratum, Geranium phaeum* var. *phaeum* 'Samobor', *Polygonatum odoratum* and *Maianthemum dilatatum* also struggled in the higher light levels initially, but they now mingle successfully to unite the lower stories of the mix. As Mix D2 has evolved *Trollius × cultorum* 'Yellow Queen' has been added for early-season interest and *Tricyrtis* 'Tojen' for late flower. We have yet to feel confident that *Heuchera villosa* and *Pulmonaria angustifolia* 'Blaues Meer' are sufficiently well-adapted to the growing conditions to be strong enough in the matrix.

1. *Trollius × cultorum* 'Yellow Queen' runs through Mix D2 in late May 2. *Actaea simplex* (Atropurpurea Group) 'Black Negligee' with *Kirengeshoma palmata* 3. *Stewartia pseudocamellia* 4. *Polygonatum odoratum* and *Maianthemum dilatatum*

Overleaf: Mix E1 transitions from the Entrance Forest into the woodland glade with *Rodgersia podophylla* and *Aruncus dioicus* var. *camschaticus* against stands of native silver birch.

1

1. *Symphyotrichum turbinellum* provides a cool contrast to the autumnal shades of *Astilbe chinensis* var. *taquetii* 'Superba' and *Stewartia pseudocamellia* 2. *Astrantia major* subsp. *involucrata* 3. *Persicaria alpina* with an underplanting of *Gillenia trifoliata* and *Tradescantia* (Andersoniana Group) 'Innocence'

3

2

Mix I

Mix I continues the damp mood of Mix H where the woodland glade meets the cantilevered central walkway. There is no woody material in this mix, but *Persicaria alpina* provides a strong signature emergent and backdrop. *Iris sanguinea* continues a vertical emergent also in Mix H along the boardwalk for early season interest, whilst *Astilbe chinensis* var. *taquetii* 'Superba' replaces the vertical in the mix with late season flower followed by seedheads that coincide with *Symphyotrichum turbinellum* in autumn. *Astrantia major* subsp. *involucrata* form a link with nearby Mix F and mingle with an understorey of *Gillenia trifoliata* and *Tradescantia* (Andersoniana Group) 'Innocence'.

1. Autumn colour of *Hakonechloa macra, Stewartia pseudocamellia* and *Symphyotrichum turbinellum* 2. *Aquilegia* 'Yellow Star' 3. Mix G2 seen across the central boardwalk 4. The lower path into the woodland glade

Overleaf: Hakonechloa macra recurs in Mixes G1 and G2 along the paths in the woodland glade. Here, in autumn, it passes through a grove of colouring Stewartia pseudocamellia.

1

2

3

Mix G2

Mixes G1 and G2 address themselves to the path edges that run through the woodland glade. The mixes are deliberately low in order to unite the pathways and provide the mixes beyond with a quiet foreground. Although woody plants appear in the mix, they are incidental and the G mixes are both shade- and sun-tolerant. The common thread through Mixes G1 and G2 is *Hakonechloa macra*. This low, Japanese grass is late to emerge, allowing for a matrix of early *Convallaria keiskei, Helleborus orientalis, Pulmonaria* 'Northern Lights' and *Brunnera macrophylla* to come before and then drop into its shadow in summer. *Pachysandra terminalis, Tiarella* 'Sugar and Spice', *Astilbe simplicifolia,* and *Cornus canadensis* are present in this early understorey, but have not competed well with the hakone grass, which has proven to be dominant. In the shadows *Houttuynia cordata,* an invasive native, has been checked by the competition of the *Hakonechloa*. Although a valuable emergent in the matrix, *Lysimachia clethroides* requires careful monitoring if it is not to overwhelm its companions in the areas that suit its preference for light. In Mix G2, *Aquilegia* 'Yellow Star', *Campanula ochroleuca* and *Euphorbia donii* 'Amjillasa' punctuate the matrix once the grass has eclipsed the earlier performers. *Fritillaria meleagris* var. *unicolor* subvar. *alba* has been added to provide an early bulb layer.

4

1

2

1. The white flowers of *Filipendula camschatica* and *Astrantia major* subsp. *involucrata* connect with the plumes of *Perscaria alpina* in Mix I beyond 2. An alpine black swallowtail butterfly feeds on *Phlox paniculata* 'David' 3. *Persicaria amplexicaulis* 'Alba', *Lilium auratum* and *Angelica gigas*

Overleaf: Angelica gigas emerges from *Persicaria amplexicaulis* 'Alba' in Mix F. The hedge of *Calamagrostis* × *acutiflora* 'Karl Foerster' jumps the main pathway to provide continuity above and below the boardwalk.

Mix F

Mix F occupies the far end of the woodland glade where it opens up into sunshine and jumps the path. It is a deliberately dramatic mix, dominated by white flowers and tall so that you move through growth that is shoulder height. The woody material is mostly peripheral, with native *Hydrangea paniculata* and *Magnolia kobus* var. *borealis* stepping from the woodland wrap for spring and then summer flower. *Rosa* 'Scharlachglut' failed and was replaced by *Salix purpurea* 'Nancy Saunders' as freestanding shrubs to screen the Kitchen Garden beyond. Native *Filipendula camschatica* is a key emergent. We replaced nursery-grown plants, which proved to be an inferior form, with plants lifted directly from the forest. Their stature provides an immediate microclimate for the matrix of perennials that move among them and over time their numbers have been reduced to diminish their bulk in the mix. *Phlox paniculata* 'David' provides scent and the tabletop aster, *Doellingeria umbellata*, a strong horizontal. A matrix of *Astrantia major* subsp. *involucrata*, *Persicaria amplexicaulis* 'Alba' and *Thalictrum aquilegiifolium* mingle among them at lower level. Japanese native *Lilium auratum* and the dark contrast of *Angelica gigas* are both self-sowing and add spontaneous verticals. *Anemone sylvestris* 'Madonna' rises early while the mix is still predominantly semi-dormant to echo the early anemone in the forest.

3

1. *Veronicastrum sibiricum*
2. *Iris sanguinea* along the boardwalk 3. *Amsonia tabernaemontana* 4. An early season view onto the matrix, the *Galium odoratum* is from neighbouring Mix D1

1

2

Mix H

Mix H runs along below the level of the main boardwalk down in the woodland glade. *Rosa glauca* and *Clematis stans* appear in the mix to provide anchor points, the rose repeating from Mix M on the other side of the boardwalk, the clematis is a signature perennial to punctuate the matrix. Mix H is designed to feel deliberately damp, with the presence of native *Iris sanguinea* marking a strong vertical. *Hosta* 'Harvest Dandy' echoes the *Hosta sieboldii* var. *rectifolia* found nearby in the forest, while *Veronicastrum sibiricum* draws upon the veronicastrum that are often found at the woodland edge. *Amsonia tabernaemontana* and *Galium odoratum* run through to provide the understorey.

3

4

Though we do not encourage too many self-seeders in the mixes to maintain stability, this biennial angelica seeds lightly enough not to be a problem. Flowering late in August with dramatic, dark plum umbels, it provides a valuable contrast to the predominance of white that is used here to give levity to the edge of the woodland.

A small number of plants jump across the main path so that there is a distinct feeling of one environment meeting and melding with another. Key to this interconnection is *Calamagrostis × acutiflora* 'Karl Foerster', which is planted in its deepest swathe on the lower levels. Here you look down onto it and can see that this is the terminus of the grassy waves that move up through the garden to make a link with the higher ground and foothills beyond. Several perennials straddle the central path to join the calamagrostis hedges in linking the lower and mid-levels together. The bright tapers of *Astilbe chinensis* var. *taquetii* 'Superba' in Mix I take the eye with colour, *Gillenia trifoliata*, with its pale gauze of flower, provides a cohesive veil and the *Veronicastrum sibiricum* nearby adds a very definite vertical. The veronicastrum is included as a visual memory of the closely related native veronicastrum that you see growing at the point where the forest meets the surrounding meadows.

Perennial meadow planting

As you enter the Meadow Garden from the bridge and move from the dappled shade of the willows and out into sunshine you are greeted by an open, light-filled atmosphere where colour is soft but constant. Gateway boulders provide a pausing spot to allow visitors the first opportunity on their journey of taking in long, open views through planting and towards the Productive Gardens. The broad meander of the central boardwalk prevents the pathway from all being seen at once and encourages visitors forward into the central part of the meadow. Here the planting marks a contrast to the woodland glade below the path and is designed to echo the way a meadow changes as it moves away from the shelter of the woodland edges and adapts to open conditions.

A solitary *Fraxinus mandshurica* var. *japonica* that predates the garden provides height at the entrance, while a number of *Rosa glauca* step out into the light and add an anchor point at mid-level. Mix M takes its lead from the *Rosa glauca*, the scale and colour soft and muted to allow the eye to travel. A light gauziness is provided by the *Gillenia trifoliata* from the damp meadow which bridges the path. Their levity and early flowering provide a veil through which the other species emerge and are softened – first the dark verticals of *Salvia nemorosa* 'Caradonna' and then a pooling of *Origanum laevigatum* as the gillenia goes over. Originally specified as *Origanum laevigatum* 'Herrenhausen', this seed-raised form of the species is paler than the named 'Herrenhausen' but provides lightness and cohesion. *Potentilla nepalensis* 'Miss Willmott' and *Campanula punctata* f. *rubriflora* 'Cherry Bells' are suspended within the origanum, while *Panicum virgatum* 'Heavy Metal' and *Agastache nepetoides* rise up as the emergents. The agastache is short-lived, but where seedlings appear with enough space to soar uninterrupted they are left alone. The high vertical they provide is important as a counterpoint to the lower-growing matrix, but is not employed to stop the eye.

A small number of the short-lived *Echinacea* 'Hot Summer' are replaced on an annual basis to provide intense pinpricks of colour near the entrance from the bridge, so that later in summer the mix retains some of the intensity provided by the earlier-flowering salvia. Wood aster, *Eurybia divaricata*, which is happy in the shadow of company, underpins the mix and provides cohesion once the origanum finishes. The wood aster – a prolific woodlander in North America – can be prone to taking over where it is combined with plants that cannot hold their own, but it is filtered through the entire central meadow to provide constancy in the late summer and autumn.

Midway through the garden, the matrix gently transitions into Mix L and *Nepeta transcaucasica* 'Blue Infinity' takes the mantle from the origanum. *Liatris spicata* and *Eryngium planum* 'Blue Glitter' provide the planting with a light-reflecting quality and feeling of dry openness. There is detail close to the path, with low perennials such as *Stachys byzantinus*, *Geranium sanguineum* and *Dianthus carthusianorum*. They demand close observation and the intricacy of the planting that sweeps close to the path in the central meadow helps to hold the visitor and provide a sense of intimacy in the very centre of the garden.

Halfway along the central walkway, the volume of the *Rosa glauca* is replaced by the height and volume of *Eupatorium maculatum* Atropurpureum Group. These powerful emergents are used in much the same way as the *Persicaria alpina* on the lower levels and their impact becomes increasingly dramatic as the season peaks in August. The gathering of height intensifies where a small path diverges from the main thoroughfare and leads towards the upper levels and the tall eupatorium provide a gateway as you move between mixes.

Mix K provides the drama here, with architectural *Eryngium agavifolium* rising up to shoulder height and creating a scene change as one moves between spaces. Early in the year, and while the eryngiums are beginning their ascent to flower, they are joined by delicate *Thalictrum* 'Splendide' and dark-leaved *Polemonium yezoense* var. *hidakanum* 'Purple Rain', a named selection of a Hokkaido native. *Persicaria amplexicaulis* 'Atrosanguinea' gathers momentum late in the season and registers as a key component to provide a sweep of intense colour and a contrast to the delicacy of the planting close to the main path. The colour is scaled up deliberately in the mix to provide the heart of the garden with a dramatic mood change from high summer onwards.

The calamagrostis hedge picks up from the lower levels of the garden and sweeps across the final third of the Meadow Garden to screen the view of the Productive Gardens beyond. Amelanchier step to either side of the calamagrostis to fray the impact of the farm buildings and reframe the mountains as you look back from the main path. As the central path leads towards the Kitchen Garden, the planting in Mix N pushes beyond the calamagrostis hedge and intensifies the pinks, the reds and the purple that run through the central meadow.

1. *Pennisetum alopecuroides* var. *viridescens* emerges in autumn to animate the garden entrance 2. *Rosa glauca* 3. *Echinacea* 'Hot Summer' 4. The first wave of colour comprises *Gillenia trifoliata* and *Salvia nemorosa* 'Caradonna' 5. *Potentilla nepalensis* 'Miss Willmott' with *Salvia nemorosa* 'Caradonna' 6. *Campanula punctata* f. rubriflora 'Cherry Bells'

Mix M

Mix M is predominantly low and softly coloured to allow the eye to travel beyond. An original *Fraxinus mandshurica* var. *japonica*, from when the garden was previously pasture, stands in isolation. *Rosa glauca* steps out from under the tree to provide volume and a foil of blue-grey foliage. *Dictamnus albus* has been slow as a feature emergent, but the vertical of *Agastache nepetoides* has compensated. *Gillenia trifoliata* provides an early, mid-storey veil of flower. *Sucissa pratensis* takes its place to create a blue haze in late season. Grey-leaved *Panicum virgatum* 'Heavy Metal', is distributed lightly through the mix and emerges late while *Pennisetum alopecuroides* var. *viridescens* around the welcome stone as a feature grass holds the entrance. The lower levels of the mingled matrix are dominated first by the vertical of *Salvia nemorosa* 'Caradonna', which blooms with the gillenia. *Origanum laevigatum, Potentilla nepalensis* 'Miss Willmott' and *Campanula punctata* f. rubriflora 'Cherry Bells' take the high summer while creamy *Eurybia divaricata* moves the mix into the autumn. Though neither *Echinacea* 'Hot Summer' nor *Digitalis ferruginea* have proven to be long-lived, they are re-introduced in small numbers annually as their unusual colour provides a welcome at the entrance to the garden.

5

6

Overleaf: In late summer *Agastache nepetoides* in Mix M and *Vernonia arkansana* 'Mammuth' in Mix J beyond add a dramatic change of scale. The blue of *Succisa pratensis* and autumnal reds of *Gillenia trifoliata* rise above *Eurybia divaricata* and *Pennisetum alopecuroides* var. *viridescens* which run throughout the matrix at the lower level.

1

Mix L

Mix L is designed to be deliberately low, addressing itself to the main path and to a small cut-through path to the upper levels of the garden. *Amelanchier canadensis* provides a light framework at the back of the mix, which is delicate and flower-rich in this central part of the garden. *Anthriscus sylvestris* 'Ravenswing' provides an early emergent, while *Echinacea pallida* and *Eryngium planum* 'Blue Glitter' rise above the matrix as later emergents. *Nepeta transcaucasica* 'Blue Infinity', *Geranium sanguineum* and the vertical spires of *Stachys byzantina* and *Liatris spicata* are key components in the mingled matrix. The running nature of *Eurybia × herveyi* has not proven to be dominant in the matrix and adds valuable high-season interest. *Dianthus carthusianorum* seeds spontaneously through the matrix, particularly towards the open conditions at the path edges.

1. *Geranium sanguineum* and *Stachys byzantina* step the mix to the path 2. *Echinacea pallida* growing with *Nepeta transcaucasica* 'Blue Infinity' 3. *Dianthus carthusianorum* 4. *Eryngium planum* 'Blue Glitter'

2

3

Overleaf: Looking through the mixes, with *Echinacea* 'Hot Summer' and *Panicum virgatum* 'Heavy Metal' of Mix M in the foreground, *Nepeta transcaucasica* 'Blue Infinity' in Mix L and *Eupatorium maculatum* Atropurpureum Group in Mix K in the midground and the lofty seedheads of *Cephalaria gigantea* in Mix C in the far distance.

4

1. *Polemonium yezoense* var. *hidakanum* 'Purple Rain'
2. *Eryngium agavifolium* with *Persicaria amplexicaulis* 'Atrosanguinea' 3. *Eryngium agavifolium* is the primary emergent 4. Mix K separated from the yellow of Mix C by a swathe of *Calamagrostis* × *acutiflora* 'Karl Foerster'

3

4

Mix K

Mix K provides a strong mood and injects both form and colour into the centre of the garden. *Amelanchier canadensis* is used sparingly throughout this area and over time will add a light framework where cross-paths bisect the garden. *Eupatorium maculatum* Atropurpureum Group marches through this area as a feature emergent and strikes a deliberate height differential to the mix that surrounds it. Early in the season, while the mix is still low, *Polemonium yezoense* var. *hidakanum* 'Purple Rain' adds early interest with *Geranium* 'Patricia'. In high summer, *Eryngium agavifolium* provides architectural vertical height, with *Thalictrum delavayi* and *Thalictrum* 'Splendide' the delicate counterpoint. *Liatris pycnostachya* injects a late-season vertical element. *Persicaria amplexicaulis* 'Atrosanguinea' feathers strong colour through this mix connecting to an adjacent run of pure persicaria, which floods the centre of the garden with late-season colour.

The native *Sanguisorba hakusanensis* is a key feature plant and, with considerable presence, it bookends the central meadow. It makes up a low percentage of Mix N and its unruly behaviour, which sees each plant taking up well over 1 sq m (1 1/4sq yd), is eased with wide spacing between plants. Flooding the free space and mingled in similar volumes are *Astrantia* 'Hadspen Blood' and *Eurybia divaricata*. *Astilbe chinensis* var. *taquetii* 'Superba' provide verticals to, and contrast with, the cascade of sanguisorba flowers, while *Valeriana officinalis* supply airiness and height.

A path running parallel to the main walkway and above it makes a third level change to define an upper part to the meadow. The smaller paths in this area echo the intimacy of those in the woodland glade, so that as you move away from the centre of the garden you are once again immersed in planting. Two important devices help change the mood here. The dramatic use of colour which is revealed as you pass between the calamagrostis hedges and a change in height intensify the experience with the step up onto higher ground. The plants are deliberately taller here so that at points you are moving through perennials that tower overhead to echo the feeling of walking among the angelica and filipendula in the forest.

The strongest colour is located here and it is more dramatic for being held back until last. Once again the calamagrostis hedges are pivotal to the reveal and the yellow colour field does not come into its greatest intensity until high summer. A hint of what is to come is provided by openly spaced groups of *Cephalaria gigantea* in Mix C, which grow to 3m (10ft) and stand clearly above the grass hedges. Once inside this upper reach of the garden and walking the intimate path system, the cephalaria are brought deliberately close to the paths so that you have to move among them. Their airy growth and transparency is also important in holding back and breaking the intensity of colour lower down at their feet. This is provided by a layer of *Coreopsis verticillata* 'Zagreb' that comes before and is then later interwoven with *Rudbeckia fulgida* var. *sullivantii* 'Goldsturm'.

Elements of simplicity are important as a counterpoint to the strength of colour. The dark *Pinus mugo* on the boundary and a simple bank of *Potentilla fruticosa* provide a resting point for the eye. A river of *Achillea* 'Coronation Gold' jumps the path and runs through the upper levels as a graphic means of pulling you through the planting as you follow its course. This registers early in the season with the silver of the achillea foliage, followed by the flare of chrome yellow and finally the darkness of the spent flower.

Thalictrum flavum subsp. *glaucum* was originally used as complimentary vertical among the cephalaria. Though hardy it has not proven to be strong on Hokkaido and has been replaced by *Thalictrum* 'Elin', which is doing better. *Digitalis lutea* and *Patrinia scabiosifolia* are used as mid-level emergents, but although *Hemerocallis esculenta* grows happily in the woodlands, it has been slow in the mix and prone to aphid out in the sunshine. It has been supplemented with the finely growing *Hemerocallis altissima* to retain the reference to the local colonies of natives.

Baptisia leucantha has been added to the yellow of mixes B and C for its mound-forming habit at mid-level. The glaucous foliage provides a contrast to the saturation of yellow and the pinnacles of pale flower are a strong vertical accent. Baptisia is a well-adapted plant here and ideal for being long-lived and reliably clump-forming.

In Japan, miscanthus are emblematic of a change in season, their flowers signifying the onset of autumn. Originally, my first drawings illustrated a bold sweep to echo the calamagrostis hedges, but I eventually decided to step *Miscanthus sinensis* 'Zebrinus' through the upper reaches of the yellow colour field in Mix C as graphic individuals with room between them to enjoy their movement. Like the switch grasses of America (*Panicum virgatum*), miscanthus have proven variable in Hokkaido as they appear the length of the country and the different forms vary dramatically in hardiness. After several trials we found 'Zebrinus' to be reliable here and, with the heat of the Hokkaido sun during summer, not so late into flower to welcome autumn. Their bright green and yellow slashed foliage also fits the colour scheme and, placed on high ground against the skyline, their plumage catches both the back light and the wind from the mountains to animate the far reaches of the autumnal garden.

Malus sieboldii act as pausing places on the upper levels of the meadow garden with seating in their shadow to shelter in the heat of summer. Over time and as they have become substantial, they have altered the mixes at their feet. Shade-lovers such as *Actaea cordifolia* in Mix A have been allowed to take control of the areas where windows in the planting have been opened up as the sun-lovers have lost vigour.

Also on the upper levels and concealed with the tall growth of Mix J and the calamagrostis hedges is a red colour field. It is the last thing you experience before you head back into the green beyond the Meadow Garden in this top corner. Colour comes early to Mix A but dims in time for the yellows that sit in the mixes alongside it not to compete. *Euphorbia griffithii* 'Fireglow' dominates the matrix both in terms of colour and the vigour of its running growth. Over time it has been reduced in density and opened up where we have plants that have not been able to withstand the euphorbia's early start. Despite its robustness, it has been worth retaining in the mix, but it does need to be teamed or managed carefully where we are introducing new plants. *Paeonia obovata*, for instance, have proved not to be strong enough, while the *Actaea cordifolia*, which are later into growth, are happy as long as they retain an open window in the mix early in the year with localized cut backs of the euphorbia.

Aruncus dioicus var. *camschaticus* and *Rosa moyesii* are used in Mix A to add volume. The creamy aruncus make a connection to those that grow in the woods and, though the rose has been slow to establish, it is rising above the dominant lowness of this matrix. *Rodgersia* 'Bronze Beauty' (a form selected and named by Omori for its brilliant spring foliage) is at its most dramatic when the euphorbia is also brightest and holds its own among it as a long-lived feature plant in the mix. *Crocosmia* 'Lucifer' and *C.* 'Hellfire' have also been successful as their foliage is able to spear through the low euphorbia to add another layer of colour.

Previous pages: The hedges of *Calamagrostis* × *acutiflora* 'Karl Foerster' provide scene changers between the mixes. *Eryngium agavifolium* and *Thalictrum* 'Splendide' identify Mix K in the mid-ground with *Persicaria amplexicaulis* 'Alba' and *Phlox paniculata* 'David' of Mix F beyond.

1

Mix N

Mix N is without a woody component. It is a deliberately simple mix with an element of drama to terminate the Meadow Garden where it meets the Kitchen Garden. *Valeriana officinalis* is an early-season emergent followed later in midsummer by a repeat of *Astilbe chinensis* var. *taquetii* 'Superba', which also features in Mix I, so that the two sides of the main path are connected. Native *Sanguisorba hakusanensis* appears in a low percentage and provides a dominant presence as a signature emergent, first with splays of grey-green foliage and then with the widely branching flower. *Astrantia* 'Hadspen Blood' and *Eurybia divaricata* mingle at low level to provide cohesion.

2

3

1. The *Valeriana officinalis* shortly before it is cut to the base to prevent it seeding with *Cephalaria gigantea* in Mix C beyond 2. *Astrantia* 'Hadspen Blood' among *Sanguisorba hakusanensis* 3. *Astilbe chinensis* var. *taquetii* 'Superba'

Overleaf: Mix C in early summer while it is still dominated by green. The swathe of *Achillea* 'Coronation Gold' that runs through this mix is just colouring with *Baptisia leucantha* in flower as an early emergent. *Cephalaria gigantea* is just rising to flower, but is still less than half its ultimate height.

1. The river of *Achillea* 'Coronation Gold' providing a focus in Mix C 2. The achillea with *Rudbeckia fulgida* var. *sullivantii* 'Goldsturm' 3. *Thalictrum* 'Elin' 4. *Hemerocallis esculenta*, a Tokachi native 5. *Cephalaria gigantea* rises above *Coreopsis verticillata* 'Zagreb'

Overleaf: Looking across Mix K to the *Miscanthus sinensis* 'Zebrinus' in Mix B and the colouring woodland wrap in mid October.

2

3

4

Mix C

Mix C provides the concentration of the yellow colour field in the upper reaches of the garden and *Pinus montana* the dark backdrop to this mix. The river of yarrow provides punctuation here as a holding point for the eye. *Miscanthus sinensis* 'Zebrinus' and *Baptisia leucantha* step into the mix to unite it with Mix B, as do the emergent verticals of *Thalictrum* 'Elin', which replaced *Thalictrum flavum* subsp. *glaucum* when it failed to do well in the climate. Lofty *Cephalaria gigantea*, in low percentage, provides a dramatic emergent and a height differential to allow the intensity of the mix an airiness against the evergreen boundary. *Coreopsis verticillata* 'Zagreb' and *Rudbeckia fulgida* var. *sullivantii* 'Goldsturm' mingle in a unifying undercurrent, the two flowering separately and then together to build intensity as the rudbeckia follows the coreopsis. The native *Hemerocallis esculenta* has been augmented with *Hemerocallis altissima*, which flowers later.

5

1. *Aruncus dioicus* var. *camschaticus* 2. *Euphorbia griffithii* 'Fireglow' 3. *Malus sieboldii* 4. *Rodgersia* 'Bronze Beauty' provides height of flower in early summer 5. In late summer *Actaea cordifolia* and *Sanguisorba officinalis* 'Red Thunder' provide the emergents and *Eurybia divaricata* low-level interest

1

2

3

Mix A

Mix A is distinct and deliberately energizing for its inclusion of orange and red. Located in the uppermost corner of the garden, it is carefully concealed by *Rosa glauca* on the lower levels so that it registers as a surprise when you come upon it. *Malus sieboldii* steps into the mix to provide shade by a seat and is joined by *Rosa glauca* and satellite *R. moyesii*, which together provide woody structure. The emergents comprise small numbers of *Aruncus dioicus* var. *camschaticus*, which provide volume, and *Sanguisorba officinalis* 'Red Thunder', which forms a red haze at shoulder height in high season. *Crocosmia* 'Lucifer' and 'Hellfire' rise above the lower growing minglers. The tall cream spears of late-flowering *Actaea cordifolia* contrast with the reds. *Rodgersia podophylla* was changed to the less invasive and more strongly coloured *Rodgersia* 'Bronze Beauty', which anchors the planting with graphic foliage. *Euphorbia griffithii* 'Fireglow'and *Eurybia divaricata* unify the mix. The euphorbia is dominant in terms of its early colour and then its growth, which is cut away from plants that might be establishing. *Paeonia obovata* was removed from the mix for its failure to compete. Small numbers of *Cirsium rivulare* 'Atropurpureum' and *Lilium pardalinum* var. *giganteum* have been added later as focal points and receive extra attention to assimilate into the community.

4

5

1

2

Mix J

Mix J sits to either side of the path where the garden steps up to the higher levels. *Malus sieboldii* and *Rosa glauca* introduce height and local shadow, but the mix is designed for open conditions. The emergents are tall so that the brightness of Mix A is screened from the main walkway. *Vernonia fasciculata* and the shorter growing *Vernonia arkansana* 'Mammuth' rise to shoulder height and taller by season's end. *Sanguisorba* 'Cangshan Cranberry' replaced the native *Sanguisorba tenuifolia* var. *alba*, which suffered from mildew in cultivation. Also tall, and used sparingly, S. 'Cangshan Cranberry' acts as a veil at high level to cast clouds of colour among the *Vernonia*. *Veronicastrum sibiricum* and the taller growing *Veronicastrum sibiricum* subsp. *yezoense* provide strong verticals. The latter, selected from local communities, adds a wilder feeling. As mid-level emergents, *Baptisia australis* provides early season colour and *Ageratina altissima* 'Chocolate' dark foliage and late-season flower. At the lower level, *Salvia nemorosa* 'Caradonna' and *Trifolium rubens* unite the matrix. Short-lived *Knautia macedonica* is allowed to self-seed to provide spontaneity and a veil of nectar-rich flower at mid-level. Native *Adenophora triphylla* var. *japonica* has self-sown from the nearby woodland into the shady areas and has now been assimilated into Mix J.

1. The differences in the two veronicastrum in Mix J can be clearly seen here 2. Short-lived *Knautia macedonica* is allowed to self-seed into niches within the mix 3. *Baptisia australis* 4. *Adenophora triphylla* var. *japonica*

3

4

Sanguisorba officinalis 'Red Thunder' introduce a summer suspension of colour at higher level once the euphorbia has dimmed to green. Their early clump-forming growth is strong enough to cope in competition as long as light can fall on the basal leaves when they are young. *Cirsium rivulare* 'Atropurpureum' and *Lilium pardalinum* var. *giganteum* appear in the matrix as emergent elements, but we have struggled to retain them among the euphorbia. Had they been introduced early while the mix was young, they may have had a chance to establish with an equal footing, but as this mix is on the edge of the garden it can afford to be simple.

Mix J provides the visual interlude between the more muted planting on the lower levels and the intensity of colour in Mix A. *Vernonia arkansana* 'Mammuth' and *Vernonia fasciculata* both appear as late-season emergents and stand bold at 2.5m (8 1/4 ft) in the mix. *Sanguisorba* 'Cangshan Cranberry', which are also tall, carry their stature more lightly with pinpricks of colour and gauziness that allow the eye to travel. *Baptisia australis* appear as early-season colour and go on to provide a mid-height volume, while *Ageratina altissima* 'Chocolate' and *Knautia macedonica* move through the lower levels among the taller emergents. Over time we have added the native *Veronicastrum sibiricum* subsp. *yezoense* to make a connection to those in the mixes that run to either side of the main path in the central section. *Adenophora triphylla* var. *japonica* has seeded into the shadowy places from the Entrance Forest and has now been included in the mix, where it has found a niche.

Opposite: Vernonia fasciculata.

Overleaf: In Mix M, a small number of *Pennisetum alopecuroides* var. *viridescens* are placed near the entrance as an autumn emergent to anchor the welcome stone.

Midori Shintani

Finding your own wild

As can be seen in the expression 'plants and trees all have something to say', the ancient Japanese revered nature and had a deep affinity with plants. In the oldest Japanese poems composed in the 8th century, we can meet our ancestors and sense that in their appreciation of plants they found the beauty of evanescence. Finding a brilliance and grace to look on flowers in full bloom, at the same time embracing a sense of transience and mutability, we find a beauty in flowers destined to fall soon. Tiny, delicate changes in sky, wind, light and every element of nature occur around us through the year. Responding sensitively to such natural phenomena, the ancient Japanese calendar of 72 seasons developed. In literature, paintings, ikebana and gardens, all Japanese art culture springs from aesthetics based on the appreciation of plants and the view of nature.

In the Millennium Forest, we cherish this traditional Japanese view of nature in nurturing our modern garden. Celebrating every stage of a plant's growth enhances the bountiful natural beauty in the garden. From shooting to flowering and then fruiting, plants show us various expressions and individualities. Our hands convey the characteristics of the plants and represent the underlying aesthetics of the garden. How to draw seasonal changes from the plant combinations has a great influence on the atmosphere of the garden. We regard the 'rustic beauty' drifting in the air of the garden. This idea is united in all our works of plant selection, plant setting, timing of seasonal maintenance, plant displays and so on.

Nurturing an eye for delicate change in plants and the season is something that I have learned from the 72 seasons. 'The earthworms rise', 'the plums turn yellow', 'white dew on the grass' – this ancient Japanese calendar lets us

Midori cuts back *Valeriana officinalis* in the Meadow Garden before it sets seed.

A cicada (semi) rests on native *Erigeron annuus*
on the woodland edge. Cicadas are the
traditional symbol of summer, which is not considered
to have started until the first one sings.

realize that we live for just a moment. The eye for the season extends to our arrangement table. We collect pieces of what we are moved by or discover in the garden and arrange flowers, foliage, fruits and vegetables to share with other people. For us, the act of arranging flowers is a dialogue with nature.

In the Meadow Garden, designed with a naturalistic planting style, the setting and quantity of each plant and the timing of maintenance are carefully determined. Especially we place emphasis on taking the balance of the planting mixes through thinning, replanting and replacing with new plants.

When we grow perennials in the garden, we sometimes meet a moment of chaos, losing structure at some point. This tends to happen in the garden with mature plants. Chaos can be romantic in the garden, but on the other hand, it very soon can look tired. We enjoy the time we have had with the plants so far and then we make a bold step change at the right time for the garden.

For example, *Sanguisorba hakusanensis* make a particular impact with their foliage in the planting in spring. As they mature, their clumps become more impressive as if big birds were resting with their wings spread out, absolutely fascinating me. But in the next phase the flowers come up and the mature plants unfold their disordered forms, making themselves vulnerable to collapse. We would like to keep them unique, but we also know that we shouldn't lose structure in one planting mix. We used to be in a dilemma here, to keep or not to keep, but as I have spent a lot of time with plants in the wild and faced natural disasters again and again, I am now able to make decisions earlier than before. Without hesitation, we make the garden fresh and get structure back by splitting old plants, replacing with new plants or encouraging colonies of next generations. Generational shifts are unceasingly processed in the nature that surrounds us. This is one of the things that I have been encouraged in by nature.

The planting is never the same. The gardener who lives every day with the garden understands its seasonal transition and delicate changes the most.

It is important for me to observe the rhythm and balance of the planting, and to clearly imagine the scenery that we will develop. 'Add an element of the wilderness to the ephemeral impression of the planting', 'Create a drama transforming from early summer into midsummer', 'Enrich different heights of plants to lift visitors' feelings' or 'Invite new plants to capture the autumn light beautifully and celebrate the last moment before winter' – such imaginations become conversations with Dan on our annual meeting later. And it returns as the vision with more enthusiastic shape to the garden by Dan, my team and myself.

The continuous observation, improvement and communication leads to the evolution of the Meadow Garden. My last 12 years with Dan have been like a journey of an insatiable adventure for a better landscape, and it continues.

I believe that everyone has a memory of touching nature. We are trying to evoke people's physical sensations and emotions experienced in nature by the naturalistic planting of the Meadow Garden. As we walk along the narrow path like an animal track, the red flowers of *Sanguisorba officinalis* will pop out and touch our shoulders and arms cheerfully. When we walk under the overwhelming height of *Cephalaria gigantea*, our hearts will pound with excitement. We will be fascinated by the fine patterns of flower buds and the gradation of delicate autumn colours in front of us. Every time we meet a plant, our minds keep moving with feelings of surprise, joy and sometimes fear. Eventually it delivers deep peace to the mind as a memory of 'the nature of the garden', and we realize that we are a part of nature. My hope is that the garden becomes a place where someone's heart returns, and where someone finds their own wild.

In the Hokkaido climate *Cephalaria gigantea*
grows to a height of 3 metres (10 feet).

WORKING THE GARDENS

Planning the year ahead

My annual visits, which occur during a different month of the growing season each year, have enabled an ongoing dialogue between Midori and myself. This openness of communication and sharing of knowledge is imperative between designer and gardener because the vision cannot be realized without a true understanding of its ethos and a united front in making it happen. Whether it be a gentle steer in the Entrance Forest or more intensive management in the Meadow Garden, we have grown to know how best to direct things through looking together and sharing an understanding of what we see and how this informs the next move.

Midori updates me with her day-to-day observations and together we decide a path for the coming year. We usually spend two days looking, walking out into the landscape and observing progress in the forest to tune the eye before circling in to walk through the gardens. The third day is spent intensively in the Meadow Garden and the stock beds, making notes and planning adjustments.

My week on site with Midori is instructive for us both, since it provides focus and objectives. We take a systematic approach in the garden, working through each planting mix and referring to the yearly notes we have made that chart the changes. Each year the balance in the garden is different, be it climatic influence or the particular life cycle of a plant. The long-lived associations are those that provide the greatest ease in terms of maintenance, but the garden also benefits from change. Since we are aiming for stability in the plantings short-lived plants are not our first choice, but we make horticultural exceptions where an accent such as *Echinacea* 'Hot Summer' might be needed to create visual interest at the entry to the garden.

The plant list totalled 80 perennials in 2008 when the garden was planted. The improvements and adjustments over the last decade have taken the numbers up to about 130. Additions to the mixes might be made on practical grounds, where we would like to extend the season or replace a plant that has not done well or has been out-competed, or for aesthetic reasons where the garden needs an accent of colour or form. All new introductions are trialled in the stock beds to prove their viability before they are introduced into the garden.

The winter on Hokkaido is long, the spring fast and the summer concentrated, with autumn having an early impact. Planning the work in the garden is consequently very much tailored to the seasons and the challenges of the climate. Whereas in the UK we can savour the winter garden by leaving it standing as there is time to prepare ahead of spring, the early snows in Hokkaido render the winter a complete downtime.

Opposite: Midori and Dan make observations during an autumn visit and consider potential adjustments to the plantings for the following year.

Overleaf: The Meadow Garden is cut back in October, ahead of the long winter, so that the rapid growth of spring is able to get away immediately after the thaw.

As the first chill winds push down from the mountains, Midori and her team start to prepare the garden for winter. Plants that have become too dominant and have been marked for removal are extracted, and the perennial meadow garden is cut to the ground with strimmers and raked in a first sweep to remove the vegetation from the growing season. The beds are cleared of any weeds that might have been missed during the summer so that the ground is clean ahead of the snow. The cleared material is composted out of visitors' range and where it would not cause risk should the bears come to forage.

Spring growth is fast and furious when it comes, so any work that can be carried out now is done so before the weather makes it impossible. The garden is mulched in the autumn using straw manure or wood manure, which is sometimes mixed with mushroom compost. The extra cover provides a degree of protection should the frosts come ahead of the snow cover. In the Rose Garden the English roses are protected against the freeze, which burns any growth that is not able to cope with the winter chill. Woody plants that do not have a track record of surviving in Tokachi, such as the *Magnolia denudata*, are provided with a traditional Japanese protective wigwam made of rice straw firmly secured against the rigours of the Hokkaido winter. We have found that if we can establish two to three years' growth without damage, the woody plants that are borderline hardy gain enough purchase to survive. Those that may require more than three years' protection are left to their own devices in the fourth year and changed or cut to the ground if they fail.

The autumn is consequently a period of much activity, and over time the team has learned where to apply their energies. Where the sasa in the forest is regenerating, swathes are cut to the ground on an annual basis to keep it in check and the litter collected to expose the seedbank again ahead of the snow. The short summer ensures that the sasa is curbed and a window of opportunity is left open for perennials growing on the forest floor. Bears hibernate under the sasa as it arches over under the weight of snow, so the areas near the paths and in the Entrance Forest are kept free of sasa to make sure that daily routes remain safe.

The winter is long and Midori and her team use this time to repair buildings, clean and store seed and perform tasks that can be useful when the landscape is dormant. Over the last few years she has also started to make trips to Taiwan to help develop the landscape and plantings at a butterfly reserve.

The slowness and longevity of winter has the effect of compressing the seasons to either side of it and by the time the winter shows signs of abating the team are hungry to start work. 'Breaking the winter' is a term that Midori uses for awakening the garden. Snow drifts and clearances that have built up over winter are shovelled as soon as there is a hint of thaw. In the garden, the snow has been vital in protecting the perennial layer beneath, but now the grip of snow cover is broken by casting powdered charcoal, which raises the surface temperature and initiates the melt. The first work starts in the forest where the native plants awaken early, far in advance of the tree canopy coming

For the first two to three years after planting new woody material, winter protection is necessary. Here *Rosa* 'Scharlachglut' is wrapped in a material traditionally woven from rice or wheat straw or rushes.

to life. Midori has established a number of forest nurseries where she has been growing stock plants in the positions that they favour. Young seedlings are introduced into these areas and left to bulk up naturally in the knowledge that they are growing unaided in the positions that suit them. There might be several years of waiting, but the spring reveals those that are mature enough to be moved into new areas where well-judged observation deems them to be suitable.

To date we have not had to replace an entire mix in the Meadow Garden, but winter damage will occasionally require areas of replacement where the snow cover has been blown away in a storm, allowing frost to penetrate deep into the ground. Division of perennials takes place in the window of April and May. Additional pot-grown plants can be added as late as June, but must go in before the race of the season speeds growth. We have had to time divisions carefully. Where, for instance, the calamagrostis hedges have tired after five or six years, there are simply not enough staff to divide all the plants at the same time, so the hedges are replenished on a staggered rotation over three years.

Where a planting might need thinning because a particular species, such as *Filipendula camschatica*, has proved to be dominant, the spring provides a second chance to recalibrate a mix. Pot-grown additions of smaller perennials that make up the same mix are added at the original spacing of 30cm (12in) between plants in areas of significant replanting. Introductions to an established mix need to be strong and in good condition, for they have a short window in which to gain a foothold alongside an already established matrix of companions. In a warm spring new plants will be watered in but, with the climate providing when it needs to, there is no irrigation in the garden. Young plants are mulched to keep the ground moist and weed-free, though no fertilizer or compost is added, keeping the mixes strong and lean.

While the garden is still low and the matrix is visible in the newly emerging foliage, the mixes are checked for balance. Plants that have a tendency to seed will reveal their progeny at this point. Seedlings are left where a new adult might be needed, but the majority are removed whenever there are signs that they might become dominant. Patterns are also exposed at this point – the direction of summer wind that will have carried the seed of a particular species in one direction, or a shaded spot where shrub cover might have changed the habitat over the course of a summer. These areas will naturally adjust, the shade-lovers in the mix taking a hold where the sun-lovers begin to fail. The success of the summer garden will be down to these spring observations and subsequent edits where the balance in the planting needs the gardener's hand to steer it back on track.

During June, the garden rears up and becomes almost impenetrable, so all spring works and weeding must be complete by this point. Strategic weeding is done with nimble removals where the cover of perennials has not been sufficient to out-compete the unwanted species. Interlopers such as *Angelica ursina* which have seeded into the garden from the forest are cut to the ground during the summer rather than dug out, to minimize disturbance. The close weave of the matrix is competitive, but if it is broken up by cultivation it becomes open to unwanted native species seeding into it.

Opposite, above: Hanging several hundred Japanese wind chimes (*furin*) in the forest to 'call the coolness' in the humid summer months. *Below:* Dan and Midori leading a summer Garden Academy in the Meadow Garden.

In mid-March, crushed
charcoal is scattered on the
snow in the Meadow Garden
to speed the thaw and
'break the winter'.

Above left and right: The shoulder seasons to either side
of winter are when the gardening team are most industrious.
Autumn preparations in October see the garden cut
back in readiness for the freeze and the many tasks that
need to happen during a rapid spring.

There is almost no staking in the garden, though as the growing season advances certain plants, such as the early-blooming *Knautia macedonica,* may be cut to the ground to promote fresh growth and so extend the garden into late summer. Paths are also kept clear with daily edits of foliage that leans uncomfortably close and impedes passage. Growth is removed on a case-by-case basis and with the same care that goes into making the arrangements on the display table. When heavy Hokkaido rains weigh down the foliage of perennials that are prone to slouching, individual plants are thinned so that the weight of the plant is lightened enough for it to lift of its own accord. This technique called *sukashi* is practised in traditional garden maintenance and marks the attention to detail that helps to keep the perennial meadow garden feeling light and lightly managed. Plants such as the baptisia and sanguisorba benefit from such care.

As the season advances, all seedheads are left to form rather than being removed. Seed that is required for the nursery is harvested for the winter and the autumnal season enjoyed for the decay and natural drawing back. It is only when the garden closes at the end of October that it is cut to the ground, cleared of debris, weeded and readied for the advance of the coming winter.

The plant laboratory

At some point during my annual visit, time is set aside to slow time. This could be a visit to Mr Izumi's forest garden to see his progress and hear more about his ongoing interaction with the environment, or Midori might take us out to visit the coastal meadows. Back at the Millennium Forest, we make time for the display table which sits under the verandah of the Garden Café. The ritual of assembling a display occurs

Above and opposite: Midori and Shintaro gather material to create a seasonal arrangement for the plant laboratory at the Garden Café.

Overleaf: The many seasons of the Japanese calendar are captured in the plant laboratory, where plants from the garden and the landscape beyond are arranged for aesthetic expression, close observation and contemplation.

almost daily during the growing season. However, it is not something that is ever rushed and Midori involves the whole team in this process of capturing the moment. The objective is to look closely, a practice that in Japan is culturally embedded in the observation of the 72 seasons of the year. Over two decades of travelling to Japan I have witnessed such celebrations on countless occasions: a kimono printed with the image of autumn leaves to capture *momiji* (Japanese maple) in the week it is at its peak: a spring tempura of petasites shoots picked from the forest or a brazier lit under the just-opening blooms of a cherry tree during the festival of *hanami*. Every five days or thereabouts a small shift is reflected in the minutiae of seasonal flux and the exercise of bringing these events into close focus brings the team closer to living with the forest.

The displays are always contemporary and though they are intimate they are free and often expressive. The ritual might see the first blossom from the crab apples marking the end of winter and the awakening of spring. With the first heat of summer, rose petals might be floated in water bowls to 'call the coolness'. Foliage, flowers and fruits are gathered from the forest, the gardens and the stock beds and in assembling them on the table, the elements are brought into new focus. The arrangements are added to and adjusted over the course of a week, building to some complexity on occasion to echo the particularity of what is happening out in the garden or the wider landscape.

The time set aside for these compositions is never seen as time that compromises what needs doing in the garden and the arrangements demonstrate an intimate awareness of the interrelated processes of looking and tending. As the season moves on, time is marked in the displays to chart the progress of the growing year. Sheaves of grass gathered one by one from rain-damaged *Calamagrostis* × *acutiflora* 'Karl Foerster' reflect both a garden that has peaked and the nurturing it takes to keep it in good condition. The sheaves gather in number as the harvest burgeons in autumn and the fruits from the garden come to join the flowers and vegetation. Midori describes the October displays as important for being 'the last time to touch green' in the gardening year.

Beyond the forest

Some years Midori arranges a Garden Academy which is open to gardeners, designers and keen amateurs who want to learn more about the principles behind the Meadow Garden. These opportunities to share what we are doing at the forest underpins the work and a day of walking and talking with the group allows us to explain the principles behind the place more deeply. We show how the gardens are influenced by the environment around us and how in turn that informs how we tend them according to naturalistic principles. We explain how the Meadow Garden is an echo of a natural environment and how the plantings aim to sit well in their place both culturally and in terms of aesthetics. The teaching is rigorous and, as well as communicating the ideas behind the gardens to others, it is very useful for focusing our ongoing work; through it, we learn never to take what we are doing for granted.

Opposite: Two plant laboratory arrangements in summer and autumn.

1

3

Since the snow precludes work in the gardens, winter jobs for the team include maintaining the traditional thatch-roofed house (*gassho-zukuri*) in the Entrance Forest which serves as the gardener's headquarters. Originally moved from Gokayama, Toyama Prefecture in Honshu, the name *gassho-zukuri* comes from the pose of joining your hands in prayer (*gassho*), which references the steep shape of the roof.

2

4

1. Gathering *Phragmites* for thatching material 2. Preparing the thatch into bundles 3. Rethatching the traditional house 4. Midori patching the roof

On the last evening of my visit Midori, Shintaro and I meet with Mr Hayashi, his sons and his management team to report on progress and discuss future plans. The owner's commitment to my yearly visit is significant and the opportunity of coming together to discuss the direction is always a point of focus. We look at the smallest details first and share our thoughts about how we find the garden. If it is a year that demands change we will discuss why and how we will effect it. If we have had change thrust upon us, as we did in the year of the typhoon, we look at how to make repairs and focus energies to bring them about quickly.

Our discussions include the future of the park and the commitment to the long-term vision, how to encourage visitors and what it takes to sustain their interest and how publicity can focus on an event such as an upcoming lecture or Garden Masterclass. We look at the ongoing photography commission with Kiichi Noro and how we might seek to use the imagery in magazine articles or book projects. The communication of the message and the aspiration for the park to thrive is an important part of forward planning.

I always raise the subject of maintenance and the importance of committing to supporting the gardeners and the team on the ground. Midori is now regularly approached by overseas students who would like the opportunity of an internship at the Millennium Forest and they have to be carefully vetted. We plan for those who will be joining in years to come and look at trips for Midori and her team and how overseas travel will benefit what we are doing in the park. We talk about lecturing opportunities, for as Midori's reputation as the head gardener at Tokachi has spread she is increasingly asked to talk internationally about the gardens. We both see our role as ambassadors for the park as an important one and it is good for the owners to hear about the reach the park has beyond its boundaries and Hokkaido.

In 2012 Fergus Garrett, Head Gardener at Great Dixter in the UK, spoke at a symposium held as part of the Hokkaido Garden Show. He was taken by the influence of the natural environment at the Millennium Forest and the synergy between the way he is managing the wilder places at Dixter with the juxtaposition of the ornamental gardens. We all saw the opportunity in the exchange of knowledge from our two worlds coming together through work experience, so Midori and I discussed the idea of setting up a gardener's exchange with him. Fergus is an impressive leader and has created a dynamic learning environment for the scholars and volunteers who come to work in the gardens.

The exchange started the following year in 2013 and works two ways. Midori and her team have travelled annually to England to gain experience of working alongside the Dixter gardeners during the Hokkaido winter. Fergus has been open about the complexities of being a head gardener, and of the logistics of running both a garden and a team simultaneously. Shintaro has broadened his own understanding of what it takes to be an Assistant Head Gardener and to provide support to the gardeners and volunteers back in Hokkaido, leading by example. The Dixter gardeners have then

1. The greenhouse is the heart of the nursery and where the majority of the plants that make their way into the garden are propagated 2. Seed saving is an essential part of the yearly maintenance regime 3. Sowing Japanese heirloom beans. There can still be frosts in June, so the plants are grown on in the greenhouse and planted out as soon as the nights are reliably mild.

1

2

3

travelled to Tokachi in the summer to learn about the Japanese approach to maintaining a naturalistic garden and Midori has been equally generous with her knowledge.

As the influence of the Millennium Forest has spread, the internships in the garden now extend beyond Great Dixter and trainees have come from Canada, the USA, the UK and Europe. They have benefited from the experience of not only working in the garden but looking at the Japanese native flora further afield on the island. A number of the garden interns have made efforts to look at the contrasting world of the Japanese gardens on Honshu and to learn about the cultural differences that exist between the Eastern and the Western approaches to the same subject.

Each year on the back of their visit to the UK, Midori and Shintaro visit like-minded gardeners, their gardens and nurseries in the UK, France and the USA. In August 2018 they made a summer trip to take part in the Beth Chatto Symposium on ecological planting, at which Midori and I had both been invited to speak. I introduced the Millennium Forest in my talk and Midori followed with a lecture that explained the Japanese connection to nature. Her talk struck a chord with the audience for its humility and the insight into *satoyama* and the art of gardening in harmony with the environment. She drew upon her knowledge of working in the forest and the steps we have made to use this understanding of a natural place to inform the way the gardens are tended.

Towards the end of a visit to the UK, Midori, Shintaro and sometimes a third member of staff come to Hillside for a few days work in the my own garden, which is run very much on naturalistic principles and is also designed to relate closely to its setting. We talk as we are working. I might explain how our meadows at Hillside are evolving as we improve their management. Midori might share an equivalent story from their management of the forest floor in Hokkaido. I will discuss how I have come to make the choices that inform the planting in at Hillside and how we might use that experience to benefit the planting in Hokkaido.

Explaining my own very personal space brings clarity to the parallel journeys we are making with the two gardens and the two very different places. Midori and her team always leave a memory of the work we have made together in the garden – a contribution to our snowdrop trail, our lavender bushes clipped perfectly or a floral display that evolved over the days of their stay which caused us to look at the familiar with refreshed eyes.

Planting takes place in spring and early summer with the growing season ahead for establishment and when it is easy to see the composition of the matrix. It takes an informed eye to understand where new plants are needed within an established planting.

Midori Shintani

The Gardenership

I made up my mind to leave Japan for Sweden to learn an unknown culture and nature when I couldn't find my direction in Japanese horticulture in my twenties. I was chaotic 'lilla japan' when I arrived in Sweden, but the nature of Scandinavia benevolently accepted me and was exceptional in guiding me to realise my vocation and my roots.

I was fortunate to be trained at the Rosendals Trädgård and the Millesgården in Stockholm, where I experienced all types of practical tasks. I learned the Scandinavian sense of beauty and understanding of design and materials, and discovered the pleasure of making a garden for everyone. Being exposed to this different culture motivated me to understand my own culture more deeply than before. After Sweden, I returned to Japan and trained to acquire various skills in traditional gardening, public park maintenance, private garden maintenance and nursery work.

During my apprenticeship in traditional Japanese gardening, as expected, I was engaged in the hardest job ever, both physically and mentally. Under the hierarchy of the rigid artisan class I learned to trust and obey the directives of the master and elder gardeners. I learned the most efficient and beautiful skills in sweeping, raking, tying traditional knots, planting moss, making tree supports and bamboo fences, pruning and even making tools. When we were setting boulders and picking up green pine needles, we always worked quietly in a tense atmosphere. Each time my fingers were calloused and couldn't move easily, I felt strong self-recrimination, as I was not yet professional.

Though strict, my training also gave me countless invaluable lessons. I learned about the tea ceremony in order to understand how to make tea gardens with

Midori Shintani and Shintaro Sasagawa prepare rose petals for the Garden Café.

1

2

3

4

1. Steven Oliver (Student Gardener, Canada)
2. Yoko Miyamura (Gardener, Tokachi Millennium Forest)
3. Midori and Shintaro with Alice Fane and
Charlie Hawkes (Student Gardeners, UK) 4. Mitsuko
Zenge (Park Manager, Japan) 5. Midori with James Horner
(Dixter gardeners exchange, UK) 6. Shintaro Sasagawa
(Assistant Head Gardener, Tokachi Millennium Forest)
7. Joshua Sparkes (Head Gardener, Forde Abbey, UK)
8. Dan, Midori and Shintaro with Mizuho Takada
(Gardener, Japan) and Noriko Yamamoto (Student
Gardener, Japan) during their apprenticeship
9. Michael Wachter (Dixter gardeners exchange, UK)
10. Elizabeth Kuhn (Nurserywoman, USA)

5

6

7

8

9

10

Above: Shintaro and Midori have built a strong partnership.
Below: Members of the Millennium Forest maintenance and garden
teams with gardeners and members of other gardens on the Hokkaido
Garden Path helping with restoration work after the 2016 typhoon.

the qualities of delicacy and hospitality, ikebana to consider plant form and seasonality and traditional culinary and religious rituals. I also found that many sublime and special places were sustained by the spirit of the gardener's self-discipline, diligence and devotion.

Since I started working at Tokachi Millennium Forest, I have come to realise the importance of what I gained through my apprenticeships. Words no longer exist in the presence of wild nature at the foot of the Hidaka Mountains. Working in silence had fostered my concentration for plants. Efficient work with minimal tools had been essential to achieving maximum vision. As most apprentices experience, true learning comes after many years of training.

As Head Gardener my further training began in 2008 and I continue to learn, to develop my team, our gardening skills, the training programme for my apprentices and student gardeners and the educational programme for our visitors. Since Shintaro Sasagawa became Assistant Head Gardener, building a strong partnership is our new challenge.

Making the garden connects people beyond its borders and now student gardeners come here from many countries. We share one forest and work together as one team. We celebrate every moment that plants give us through the seasons. As I had before, the students come into contact with a different culture and experience the joy of being connected to an unfamiliar nature.

The Tokachi Millennium Forest has been nurtured by a lot of people. Our gardening hands might only be a moment in the eternally continuous forest time, but it is the accumulation of precious moments that everyone has given. I truly believe that it will breathe in the future forest and will be alive in the gardeners themselves.

ENDNOTE

Hillside and back to nature

My work has always looked to the natural world first, to the environment and the interaction of the place and the way the plants grow there. It has been an evolution that started early with field trips to look at natural plant communities in my late teens and played out in my first large-scale commission of Home Farm in Northamptonshire in my early twenties. Having trained as a gardener, it was important to be able to put my observations that nature be the guide into practice and it was necessary to live through the process of developing these ideas in the 14 years I looked after the garden.

So, it was a remarkable opportunity to be able to work at scale and with a mission to re-engage people with nature through the gardens and their setting at the Millennium Forest. My time spent with the forest has been a huge influence, not least because it has given me the opportunity to engage with such a remarkable flora in Hokkaido but also the very nature of the project, with its beyond-our-lifetime view, has made me think bigger. Working at a scale that involves physically making your way into a landscape and learning to think with an expansive time frame reminds us that we are just a tiny part of this environment, but the gardens have allowed us to make a way into it. By seeing how things tick, learning from the natural orders and humbling ourselves to respect them, we can be more in balance and insightful.

My partner Huw and I moved to Somerset a decade ago with the specific aim of becoming part of a landscape. Over the last decade our 8 hectares (20 acres) at Hillside have allowed me to play out this relationship with a piece of land for myself. It is a scale that is bigger than one I can possibly manage in entirety, but living here allows an interaction at close quarters and on a day-to-day basis. Engaging in the process of refining this place has given me the opportunity to test my ideas and my resolve to steer an ever-lighter touch on the land with the aim of giving it its rein and learning from the natural orders. It has helped me to use my skills as a gardener and landscape designer and to craft a dialogue with nature that aims for balance and biodiversity.

Through managing the land in this way, we have become more aware of the power of our influence and to think before we act. Our mission at Hillside is to strike a balance between gardening only as much as we need to and nurturing the land to steer its evolution where the boundaries are less defined. The ripples of influence have more energy closer to the buildings and dissipate progressively in a series of environments that finger outwards into the landscape. We grow to eat from an organic kitchen garden and an orchard planted close to the buildings. We have made an ornamental garden here too which draws upon the influence of the 'wilder' places we have been managing

beyond the boundaries of what we cannot physically garden. The managed meadows and the rough places we are allowing to revert from pasture back to woodland provide a litmus and an ever-expanding ecology. The wild, wet ditches are my place for experimentation, to manage the land in the way we do at the forest to reveal its best and most interesting attributes.

The garden close to the house is an enriched environment. It is layered and complex like the communities of plants in the meadows and ditches that inspired it but it also represents a personal evolution of gardening ever more loosely, imposing only so much control as is necessary to allow the plant community its play. We have learned through the day-to-day tending at Hillside that it is not a case of the garden versus the environment but the synergy between the two where the richness happens.

Learning about the art of *satoyama* over the last 20 years of working at the Millennium Forest has been a privilege, and we have been practising our own version at Hillside quite intuitively. We work the land intensively where required but take only as much as we need from it: food from the vegetable garden, materials from the coppice and wild pickings from the wood and hedgerows. The influence of Japan has been potent. We have learned to prize the small, fleeting occurrences and have developed a language of appreciating them more fully, flowers or fruit picked and savoured; conversely, we take time with a repetitive task and allow the experience to deepen for not rushing it. The way of seeing through wabi and sabi has shown us how to value the underplayed and the modest, the kind of quiet, undeclared beauty that waits patiently to be discovered. The collective experience is one that has a positive influence over the way we live and through tending the land we have learned to know our place as custodians of this environment.

Previous pages: Midori and Shintaro rake the forest floor in autumn ahead of the first snowfall.

Above: The garden at Hillside gives way seamlessly to landscape, the one informing the other and the boundary between the two being deliberately blurred.

THE PLANT MIXES

The Meadow Garden was originally planted in 2008. The plant mixes have
been adjusted in a gradual process over the years to respond to cultural and aesthetic
demands. In places where a mix has bridged a path or responded to the evolving
woody layer for instance, it has been subdivided to reflect the differences. We now
treat each subdivision as a variant to reflect the change in their dynamic.
For example Mix D1+ is a variant of the original Mix D.

Original plants	Additions	Removed/Failed
MIX A		
Trees & Shrubs	*Actaea cordifolia* (2009)	*Rodgersia podophylla* (2011)
Malus sieboldii	*Rodgersia* 'Bronze Beauty' (2011)	*Paeonia obovata* (2012)
Rosa glauca	*Rosa moyesii* (2012)	
Rosa moyesii	*Cirsium rivulare* 'Atropurpureum' (2013)	
Perennials	*Lilium pardalinum* var. *giganteum* (2013)	
Aruncus dioicus var. *camschaticus*	*Sanguisorba officinalis* 'Red Thunder' (2014)	
Eurybia divaricata	*Crocosmia* 'Lucifer' (2016)	
Euphorbia griffithii 'Fireglow'	*Crocosmia* 'Hellfire' (2017)	
Paeonia obovata	**Future**	
Rodgersia podophylla	*Cirsium canum*	
	Cirsium rivulare 'Trevor's Blue Wonder'	
	Paeonia mlokosewitschii	
	Paeonia 'Scarlet O'Hara'	
MIX B		
Alchemilla mollis	*Asclepias incarnata* 'Soulmate' (2010)	*Thermopsis lupinoides* (2009)
Levisticum officinale	*Miscanthus sinensis* 'Zebrinus' (2010)	*Levisticum officinale* (2014)
Ligularia 'The Rocket'	*Baptisia leucantha* (2011)	
Rudbeckia fulgida var. *sullivantii* 'Goldsturm'	*Peucedanum verticillare* (2011)	
Sanguisorba albiflora	*Thalictrum* 'Elin' (2013)	
Thermopsis lupinoides	*Verbascum* 'Christo's Yellow Lightning' (2013)	
	Digitalis lutea (2014)	
	Patrinia scabiosifolia (2014)	
	Future	
	Angelica perennial sp.	
	Paeonia mlokosewitschii	
MIX C		
Cephalaria gigantea	*Miscanthus sinensis* 'Zebrinus' (2010)	*Thermopsis lupinoides* (2009)
Coreopsis verticillata 'Zagreb'	*Baptisia leucantha* (2011)	
Hemerocallis esculenta	*Peucedanum verticillare* (2011)	
Rudbeckia fulgida var. *sullivantii* 'Goldsturm'	*Hemerocallis altissima* (2013)	
Thalictrum flavum subsp. *glaucum*	*Thalictrum* 'Elin' (2013)	
Thermopsis lupinoides	*Digitalis lutea* (2014)	
	Patrinia scabiosifolia (2014)	
MIX D1		
Trees and shrubs	*Sambucus nigra* 'Black Lace' (2009)	*Sambucus nigra* 'Black Lace' (2012)
Existing *Fraxinus*	*Aralia elata* (2011)	
Cercidiphyllum japonicum	*Rosa sericea* subsp. *omeiensis* f. *pteracantha* (2012)	
Fraxinus mandshurica var. *japonica*	*Iris chrysographes* 'Black Form' (2014)	
Perennials		
Actaea simplex (Atropurpurea Group) 'Black Negligee'		
Galium odoratum		
Geranium phaeum var. *phaeum* 'Samobor'		
Kirengeshoma palmata		
Polygonatum odoratum		

Original plants	Additions	Removed/Failed
MIX D1+		

Trees and shrubs
Aralia elata
Cercidiphyllum japonicum

Perennials
Actaea simplex (Atropurpurea Group) 'Black Negligee'
Galium odoratum
Geranium phaeum var. *phaeum* 'Samobor'
Kirengeshoma palmata
Polygonatum odoratum

	Additions	Removed/Failed
	Sambucus nigra 'Black Lace' (2009)	*Kirengeshoma palmata* (2011)
	Aralia elata (2011)	*Sambucus nigra* 'Black Lace' (2012)
	Magnolia denudata (2011)	*Magnolia denudata* (2015)
	Rosa sericea subsp. *omeiensis* f. *pteracantha* (2012)	
	Iris × *robusta* 'Gerald Darby' (2013)	
	Symphyotrichum turbinellum (2014)	
	Thalictrum delavayi 'Album' (2015)	

MIX D2

Trees and shrubs
Aralia elata
Stewartia pseudocamellia

Perennials
Actaea simplex (Atropurpurea Group) 'Black Negligee'
Hydrangea paniculata
Kirengeshoma palmata
Maianthemum dilatatum
Polygonatum odoratum
Tricyrtis 'Tojen'

Future
Lilium 'Claude Shride'
Lilium × *dalhansonii*

MIX D2+

Trees and shrubs
Aralia elata
Stewartia pseudocamellia

Perennials
Actaea simplex (Atropurpurea Group) 'Black Negligee'
Kirengeshoma palmata
Maianthemum dilatatum
Polygonatum odoratum
Tricyrtis 'Tojen'

	Additions	Removed/Failed
	Persicaria alpina (2009)	*Kirengeshoma palmata* (2010)
	Sambucus nigra 'Black Lace' (2009)	*Sambucus nigra* 'Black Lace' (2012)
	Trollius × *cultorum* 'Yellow Queen' (2011)	*Lilium henryi* (2017)
	Rosa sericea subsp. *omeiensis* f. *pteracantha* (2012)	
	Symphyotrichum turbinellum (2012)	
	Chasmanthium latifolium (2013)	
	Selinum wallichianum (2013)	
	Deschampsia cespitosa 'Goldtau' (2014)	
	Heuchera villosa (2015)	
	Lilium henryi (2015)	
	Pulmonaria angustifolia 'Blaues Meer' (2015)	

Future
Actaea simplex (Atropurpurea Group) 'James Compton'
Iris 'Berlin Tiger'

MIX E1

Trees and shrubs
Aralia elata
Stewartia pseudocamellia

Perennials
Anemone hupehensis var. *japonica*
Aruncus dioicus var. *camschaticus*
Rodgersia podophylla
Trillium camschatcense
Veratrum nigrum

	Additions	Removed/Failed
	Paeonia obovata 2011	*Paeonia obovata* (2015)
	Hydrangea serrata var. *megacarpa* (2012)	
	Lamprocapnos spectabilis 'Alba' (2013)	
	Paeonia lactiflora 'White Wings' (2013)	
	Iris chrysographes (2014)	
	Thalictrum delavayi 'Album' (2014)	
	Camassia leichtlinii 'Alba' (2015)	
	Fritillaria meleagris (2015)	
	Galanthus elwesii (2015)	
	Galium odoratum (2016)	
	Geranium phaeum var. *phaeum* 'Samobor' (2016)	
	Veratrum maackii (2017)	

Future
Maianthemum japonica
Thalictrum Splendide White = 'Fr21034'

MIX E2

Trees and shrubs
Hydrangea paniculata

Perennials
Artemisia lactiflora Guizhou Group
Astilbe thunbergii var. *congesta*
Matteuccia struthiopteris
Tellima grandiflora

	Additions	Removed/Failed
		Artemisia lactiflora Guizhou Group (2013)

Original plants	Additions	Removed/Failed
MIX F		
Trees and shrubs	*Rosa* 'Scharlachglut' (2010)	*Rosa* 'Scharlachglut' (2018)
Hydrangea paniculata	*Phlox paniculata* 'David' (2011)	*Artemisia lactiflora* Guizhou Group (2014)
Magnolia kobus var. *borealis*	*Artemisia lactiflora* Guizhou Group (2013)	
Salix purpurea 'Nancy Saunders'	*Angelica gigas* (2014)	
	Doellingeria umbellata (2017)	
Perennials		
Anemone sylvestris 'Madonna'	**Future**	
Astrantia major subsp. *involucrata*	*Aconitum* 'Sparks Variety'	
Filipendula camschatica	*Aconitum* 'Stainless Steel'	
Lilium auratum	*Cenolophium denudatum*	
Persicaria amplexicaulis 'Alba'	*Eupatorium fistulosum* f. *albidum* 'Ivory Towers'	
Thalictrum aquilegiifolium	*Salix purpurea* 'Nancy Saunders'	
MIX G1		
Trees and shrubs	*Hydrangea serrata* var. *megacarpa* (2012)	*Cornus kousa* 'Chinensis'
Aralia elata		
Stewartia pseudocamellia		
Perennials		
Convallaria keiskei		
Cornus canadensis		
Hakonechloa macra		
Houttuynia cordata		
Pulmonaria 'Northern Lights'		
MIX G2		
Trees and shrubs	*Aquilegia* 'Yellow Star' (2010)	*Pachysandra terminalis* (2010)
Malus sieboldii	*Astilbe simplicifolia* (2010)	*Astilbe simplicifolia* (2012)
	Campanula ochroleuca (2015)	
Perennials	*Fritillaria meleagris* var. *unicolor* subvar. *alba* (2015)	
Brunnera macrophylla	*Euphorbia donii* 'Amjillasa' (2017)	
Hakonechloa macra		
Helleborus orientalis	**Future**	
Lysimachia clethroides	*Pulmonaria* 'Blue Ensign'	
Pachysandra terminalis		
Tiarella 'Sugar and Spice'		
MIX H		
Trees and shrubs	*Clematis stans* (2017)	
Rosa glauca		
Perennials		
Amsonia tabernaemontana		
Hosta 'Harvest Dandy'		
Iris sanguinea		
Veronicastrum sibiricum		
MIX I		
Astilbe chinensis var. *taquetii* 'Superba'	*Persicaria alpina* (2009)	
Astrantia major subsp. *involucrata*	*Symphyotrichum turbinellum* (2014)	
Gillenia trifoliata		
Iris sanguinea		
Tradescantia (Andersoniana Group) 'Innocence'		
MIX J		
Trees and shrubs	*Sanguisorba tenuifolia* var. *alba* (2010)	*Sanguisorba tenuifolia* var. *alba* (2015)
Malus sieboldii	*Veronicastrum sibiricum* subsp. *yezoense* (2012)	*Veronicastrum sibiricum* (2017)
Rosa glauca	*Vernonia arkansana* 'Mammuth' (2014)	*Trifolium rubens* (2018)
	Vernonia fasciculata (2014)	
Perennials	*Sanguisorba* 'Cangshan Cranberry' (2015)	
Baptisia australis	*Trifolium rubens* (2015)	
Knautia macedonica	*Ageratina altissima* 'Chocolate' (2017)	
Salvia nemorosa 'Caradonna'	*Adenophora triphylla* var. *japonica* (2018)	
Veronicastrum sibiricum		

Original plants	Additions	Removed/Failed

MIX K

Trees and shrubs
Amelanchier canadensis

Thalictrum Splendide White = 'Fr21034' (2014)
Liatris pycnostachya (2015)

Perennials
Eryngium agavifolium
Eupatorium maculatum Atropurpureum Group
Geranium 'Patricia'
Persicaria amplexicaulis 'Atrosanguinea'
Polemonium yezoense var. *hidakanum* 'Purple Rain'
Thalictrum delavayi

Future
Liatris spicata

MIX L

Trees and shrubs
Amelanchier canadensis

Nepeta transcaucasica 'Blue Infinity' (2009)
Eryngium planum (2012)
Echinacea pallida (2013)
Aster diplostephioides (2014)
Hylotelephium 'Jose Aubergine' (2014)
Eryngium planum 'Blue Glitter' (2015)
Eurybia × *herveyi* (2016)
Stipa barbata (2016)
Anthriscus sylvestris 'Ravenswing' (2018)
Liatris spicata (2018)

Eryngium planum (2014)
Hylotelephium 'Jose Aubergine' (2017)
Limonium platyphyllum (syn. *L latifolium*) (2009)
Aster diplostephioides (2015)
Stipa barbata (2018)

Perennials
Dianthus carthusianorum
Geranium sanguineum
Limonium platyphyllum (syn. *L latifolium*)
Stachys byzantina

Future
Centaurea montana 'Lady Flora Hastings'

MIX M

Trees and shrubs
Malus sieboldii
Rosa glauca

Campanula punctata f. *rubriflora* 'Cherry Bells' (2010)
Agastache nepetoides (2011)
Pennisetum alopecuroides var. *viridescens* (2011)
Echinacea 'Hot Summer' (2013)
Panicum virgatum 'Heavy Metal' (2013)
Digitalis ferruginea (2014)
Panicum virgatum 'Cloud Nine' (2014)
Succisa pratensis (2016)

Perennials
Eurybia divaricata
Dictamnus albus
Gillenia trifoliata
Origanum laevigatum
Potentilla nepalensis 'Miss Willmott'
Salvia nemorosa 'Caradonna'

Future
Succisa pratensis 'Derby Purple'
Gladiolus 'Ruby'

MIX N

Astilbe chinensis var. *taquetii* 'Superba'
Astrantia 'Hadspen Blood'
Eurybia divaricata
Valeriana officinalis

Sanguisorba hakusanensis 2010

Future
Aster trifoliatus subsp. *ageratoides* 'Ezo Murasaki'

Woodland wrap
Betula platyphylla
Enkianthus campanulatus
Euonymus hamiltonianus
Hydrangea arborea
Magnolia kobus
Pinus montana
Quercus mongolica subsp. *crispula*
Rhododendron brachytricum
Rosa rugosa
Salix alba var. *sericea*
Sorbaria sorbifolia
Sorbus commixta

Perennial swathes
Achillea 'Coronation Gold'
Calamagrostis × *acutiflora* 'Karl Foerster'
Potentilla fruticosa

RESOURCES

Websites

Hokkaido Garden Path
hokkaido-garden.jp/english/

The Ainu Museum
ainu-upopoy.jp/en/

Akarenga – Portal Site of
Hokkaido's History and Culture
akarenga-h.jp/en/

Untouched Hokkaido
untouchedhokkaido.jp/en/

Books and Articles

Aesthetics

Koren, Leonard, *How to Rake Leaves*
(Stone Bridge Press, Albany, CA, 1993)
— *How to Take a Japanese Bath* (Stone
Bridge Press, Albany, CA, 2018)
—*Undesigning the Bath* (Stone Bridge
Press, Albany, CA, 1996)
— *Wabi-sabi: For Artists, Designers,
Poets & Philosophers* (Imperfect
Publishing, Point Reyes, CA, 2008)
— *Wabi-sabi: Further Thoughts*
(Imperfect Publishing, Point Reyes,
CA, 2015)

Nobuyoshi, Hamada, *The Traditional
Colors of Japan* (PIE International,
Tokyo, 2015)

Richie, Donald, *A Lateral View: Essays
on Culture and Style in Contemporary
Japan* (Stone Bridge Press, Berkeley,
CA, 1998)
— *A Tractate on Japanese Aesthetics*
(Stone Bridge Press, Albany, CA, 2007)

Takahiko, Sano, and Nobuyoshi,
Hamada, *Traditional Japanese Color
Palette* (PIE International, Tokyo, 2015)

Tanizaki, Junichiro, *In Praise of
Shadows* (Vintage Classics, London,
2001)

General history

Kerr, Alex, *Lost Japan*
(Penguin, London, 2015)

Richie, Donald, *The Inland Sea*
(Stone Bridge Press, Albany, CA, 2009)

Gardens and plants

Ito, Teiji, *The Gardens of Japan*
(Kodansha, Tokyo, 1984)

Koren, Leonard, *Gardens of Gravel and
Sand,* (Stone Bridge Press, Albany, CA,
2009)

Levy-Yamamori, Ran and Taaffe,
Gerard, *Garden Plants of Japan* (Timber
Press, Portland, OR, 2004)

Walker, Sophie, *The Japanese Garden*
(Phaidon, London, 2017)

The Ainu

Katsuichi, Honda, *Harukor: An Ainu
Woman's Tale* (University of California
Press, Berkeley, CA, 2000)

Landor, Arnold Henry Savage, *Alone
with the Hairy Ainu: Or, 3,800 Miles
on a Pack Saddle in Yezo and a Cruise
to the Kurile Islands* CreateSpace
Independent Publishing Platform

Peterson, Benjamin (trans.), *The Song
The Owl God Sang: The collected Ainu
legends of Chiri Yukie* (BJS Books, 2013)

Shigeru, Kayano, *Our Land Was a
Forest: An Ainu Memoir* (Westview
Press, Boulder, CO, 1994)

— *The Ainu: History, Culture and
Folktales* (Tuttle Publishing, North
Clarendon, VT, 2004)

Walker, Brett L., *The Conquest of Ainu
Lands: Ecology and Culture in Japanese
Expansion, 1590–1800* (University of
California Press, Berkeley, CA, 2006)

Satoyama

Duraiappah, Anantha Kumar (Ed),
Nakamura, Koji (Ed), Takeuchi,
Kazuhiko (Ed), Watanabe, Masataka
(Ed), Nishi, Maiko (Ed), *Satoyama-
Satoumi Ecosystems and Human
Well-Being: Socio-Ecological Production
Landscapes of Japan* (United Nations
Publications, New York, 2012)

Takeuchi, K. (Ed), Brown, R. (Ed),
Washitani, I. (Ed), Tsunekawa, A.
(Ed), Yokohari, M. (Ed), *Satoyama: The
Traditional Rural Landscape of Japan*
(Springer Publishing, New York, 2003)

Shinto

Ono, Sokyo, *Shinto, The Kami Way*
(Tuttle Publishing, North Clarendon
VT, 2004)

Wabi and sabi

Andō, Tadao, "What Is Wabi-Sabi?"
accessed 20 May 2020
http://nobleharbor.com/tea/chado/
WhatIsWabi-Sabi.htm

Zen

Suzuki, Daisetz T., *Zen and Japanese
Culture* (Princeton University Press,
Princeton and Oxford, 2010)

Television

Satoyama: Japan's Secret Water Garden,
narrated by David Attenborough
(NHK, 2004)

*Opposite: Rosa 'Munstead
Wood' in an antique vase
belonging to Midori.*

INDEX

Page numbers in *italic* type refer to pictures.

A

Achillea 'Coronation Gold' *165*, 214, *218–19*, 220, *220*, 277
Aconitum
  gigas 86
  sachalinense subsp.
  yezoense *78, 79*
    'Sparks Variety' 276
    'Stainless Steel' 276
Actaea
  cordifolia 215, *225*, 274
  simplex (Atropurpurea Group) 'Black Negligee' *157*, *179*, 181, *184*, *185*, 274, *275*
  simplex (Atropurpurea Group) 'James Compton' 275
Actinidia 78
Adenophora triphylla var. *japonica* *226*, *227*, 228, 276
Aesculus turbinata *2*
Agastache nepetoides *174–5*, 200–1, *202*, *204–5*
Ageratina altissima 'Chocolate' *226*, 226, 228, 276
agriculture 22, 30, 31, 41, 44, 46, 47, 49, 53, 94, 103, 119
  impact on natural vegetation 53–4, 55
Ainu 21, 29, 35, 53, 78, 119
aki-karamatsu *84–5*
akitabuki *84–5*
Alchemilla mollis 274
alder 103
Allium victorialis subsp. *platyphyllum* 143
Amaranthus 125, *126–7*
Amelanchier canadensis 206, 210, 277
Amsonia tabernaemontana *198*, *199*, 276
Anemone 69, 78, *169*, 172
  flaccida *82*, 97
  hupehensis var. *japonica* 275
  sylvestris 'Madonna' 181, *194*, 276

Angelica 172, 274
  edulis 181
  gigas 181, *194*, *195*, *196–7*, 200, 276
  ursina *30*, 45, *63*, 247
Anthriscus sylvestris 'Ravenswing' 206, 277
Aquilegia
  oxysepala 86
  'Yellow Star' 190, *190*, 276
Aralia
  cordata 143
  elata 160, *161*, 178, *179*, 180, 274, *275*, 276
Arisaema *169*
  serratum 86
art trail 58
Artemisia
  indica var. *maximowiczii* 140
  lactiflora Guizhou Group *275*, 276
Aruncus dioicus var. *camschaticus* *76–7*, *81*, *186–7*, 215, 224, *224*, 274, 275
Asano, Osamu 58
Asclepias incarnata *173*
  'Soulmate' 274
Aster
  diplostephioides 277
  trifoliatus subsp. *ageratoides* 'Ezo Murasaki' 277
Astilbe
  chinensis var. *taquetii* 'Superba' *188*, *189*, 200, 214, 216, 217, 276, 277
  simplicifolia 190, 276
  thunbergii var. *congesta* 275
Astrantia
  'Hadspen Blood' 214, 216, *217*, 277
  major subsp. *involucrata* *168*, 181, *188*, 189, *194*, *194*, 276
asymmetry in Japanese gardens 64

B

baikeiso *83*, *86*, *91*
Bando, Masaru
  Circle of Kamui 103, 104
Baptisia 156, 252
  australis *158–9*, *226*, *227*, 228, 276

  leucantha 215, *218–19*, 220, 274
bears 41, 75, 78, 90
Betula platyphylla *20*, *30*, 75, 97, 177, *186–7*, 277
biodiversity *36–7*, 44, 52, 53, 59, 75
  re-establishing 55
blueberry 145
bogs 40
bonsai 17
Brunnera macrophylla 190, 276

C

Calamagrostis × *acutiflora* 'Karl Foerster' *161*, 164, 172, 176, *196–7*, 200, *210–13*, 215, 247, 256, 277
Caltha 78
  palustris 40
  palustris var. *barthei* *40*, 83
Camassia *120–1*
  leichtlinii 'Alba' 275
Campanula
  ochroleuca 190, 276
  punctata f. *rubriflora* 'Cherry Bells' 200, 202, *202*
Cardiocrinum 172
  cordatum var. *glehnii* 78, *80*
Carex 172
Cenolophium denudatum 276
Centaurea montana 'Lady Flora Hastings' 277
Cephalaria gigantea *208–9*, 214, *216–17*, *218–19*, 220, *220*, *236*, *237*, 274
Cercidiphyllum japonicum *161*, 178, 180, 274, 275
Chasmanthium latifolium 275
chishima-azami *92–3*
cicadas 78
Circle of Kamui *60–1*, 103, 104
Cirsium
  canum 274
  kamtschaticum *92–3*
  rivulare 'Atropurpureum' 224, 228, 274
  rivulare 'Trevor's Blue Wonder' 274
Clark, William Smith 29
Clematis stans 198, 276
climate 29, 35, *36–9*, 40–1, 44, 119, 139, 241–52, 245
companion planting 118
Convallaria keiskei 190, 276

coppicing 47, 97
Coreopsis verticillata 'Zagreb' *165*, 214, 220, 221, 274
Cornus
  canadensis 190, 276
  kousa 'Chinensis' 276
Corydalis
  ambigua 83
  cordata 97
Courbot, Didier 58
Crocosmia
  'Hellfire' 215, 224, 274
  'Lucifer' 215, 224, 274
Cutting Garden *126–7*, 129

D

Dahlia 125, *126–7*
David Austin Roses 134, 139
Deschampsia cespitosa 'Goldtau' 275
Dianthus carthusianorum 206, 207, 277
Dictamnus albus 202, 277
Digitalis
  ferruginea 202
  lutea 214, 274
Doellingeria umbellata *194*, 276

E

Earth Garden *9*, *18–19*, *24–5*, 40, *60–1*, 65, 68, 75, *100–1*, *102*, *103–14*, 105, 106, *108–13*, 115, 149
Echinacea
  'Hot Summer' *173*, 201, 202, *202*, *208–9*, 241
  pallida 206, 207, 277
education programme 58, 246, 256
elegance, Japanese concept of 8
Enkianthus campanulatus 277
Entrance Forest 54, 58, 59, *60–1*, 64, 68, 74, 75, *76–7*, 78, *79*, 90, 97, 98
  traditional Japanese building *258–9*
Erigeron annuus 234
Eryngium
  agavifolium 210, *210*, *212–13*, 277
  planum 277
  planum 'Blue Glitter' 206, 207, 277
Euonymus hamiltonianus 277

Eupatorium
    fistulosum f. *albidum* 'Ivory
      Towers' 276
    maculatum Atropurpureum
      Group 165, 208–9, 210, 277
Euphorbia 228
    donii 'Amjillasa' 190, 276
    griffithii 'Fireglow' 164, 215,
      224, 224, 274
Eurybia
    divaricata 164, 201, 202,
      204-5, 214, 216, 225, 274, 277
    × *herveyi* 174–5, 206, 277
ezo-no-reijinso 86
ezo-no-ryukinka...83
ezo-no-shimotsukeso 76–7, 87
ezo-torikabuto 79
ezoengosaku 83
ezonyu 45

F

Fallopia 90
    sachalinensis 30, 92–3
Filipendula 69, 172
    camschatica 168, 173, 181,
      194, 194, 247, 276
    glaberrima 76–7, 87
forage plants 84–5, 90, 119,
    142, 143–4
Forest Garden 23, 60–1, 75,
    88–9, 90, 94–8, 99
forest management 75–98
forest nurseries 90, 94, 247
formality in Japanese gardens
    64
Fraxinus 274
    mandshurica var. *japonica*
      200, 202, 274
Fritillaria meleagris 275
    var. *unicolor* subvar. *alba*
      190, 276
fuki 142, 143
Fukui 44, 46
furin 15, 246

G

Galanthus elwesii 275
Galium odoratum 157, 182–3,
    184, 198, 199, 274, 275
Garden Academy 246, 256
Garden Café 60–1, 119, 125,
    128, 130–1, 143–4, 252
Garden Masterplan 58–65,
    60–1, 68, 103
Garrett, Fergus 9, 70, 260

gassho-zukuri 258–9
genius loci 64
Geranium
    'Patricia' 210, 277
    phaeum var. *phaeum*
      'Samobor' 157, 179, 181, 184,
      274, 275
    sanguineum 206, 206–7,
      277
Gillenia trifoliata 160, 164,
    188–9, 189, 200, 202,
    202, 204–5, 276, 277
Glaucidium palmatum 82, 90
Goat Farm 58, 60–1, 68, 119,
    149
grassland 58
Great Dixter/Dixter gardeners
    exchange 9, 70, 260, 263,
    266

H

Hakonechloa macra 173, 181,
    190, 190, 192–3, 276
hanami 15, 17, 256
haru-karamatsu 87
Hayashi, Hiroshi 71
Hayashi, Katsuhiko 71
Hayashi, Mitsushige 8, 11,
    21–2, 35, 53, 54, 68,
    70, 71, 103, 260
Helianthus salicifolius 172
Helleborus orientalis 181, 190,
    276
Hemerocallis 169
    altissima 214, 220, 274
    esculenta 66–7, 214, 220,
      220, 274
Heuchera villosa 184, 275
Hidaka Mountains 6–7, 22, 30,
    31, 32–3, 35, 53, 56–7, 58,
    60–1, 65, 68, 104, 107
    shakkei 65, 104, 107, 149,
    176–7
Hokkaido 16, 21, 28, 29–30, 94
    climate 29, 35, 36–9, 40–1,
      44, 119, 139, 241–52, 245
Hokkaido Garden Path 119, 132
Hokkaido Garden Show 60–1,
    75, 90, 97, 260
horse paddocks 60–1, 75, 78,
    94, 103
horse riding 24–5, 58, 75
hoshigaki 143
Hosta 169, 181

'Harvest Dandy' 198, 276
    sieboldii var. *rectifolia* 87,
      198
Houttuynia cordata 173, 190,
    276
Hydrangea
    arborea 277
    paniculata 168, 194, 275, 276
    petiolaris 78
    serrata var. *megacarpa* 180,
      275, 276
hydroseeding 106, 107
Hylotelephium 'Jose Aubergine'
    277
Hypericum ascyron 87

I

immersive planting 65
indigenous species 59, 63, 65,
    68, 97, 169, 172, 173, 177, 180,
    194, 247
    residual seedbank 54, 59,
      88–9
industrialization 48
intimacy 58
Iris
    'Berlin Tiger' 275
    chrysographes 275
    chrysographes 'Black Form'
      274
    × *robusta* 'Gerald Darby'
      178, 181, 184, 275
    sanguinea 181, 189, 198,
      198–9, 276
Izumi, Yukihiro 59, 63, 252

J

Japanese cedar 48
Japanese cypress 48
Japanese gardens 14, 15–16

K

kami 47
katsura 180
kurumaba-tsukubaneso...83
Kirengeshoma palmata 157,
    180–1, 184, 185, 274, 275
Kisara Building 58, 60–1, 149
Kitchen Garden 116–18, 119,
    124, 125, 128–31, 140–4, 141,
    142, 143, 144, 145, 152
Knautia macedonica 169, 173,
    226, 226, 228, 252, 276
koraitennansho 86
Kuhn, Elizabeth 267

kumazasa 20
kurumayuri 86
kusasotetsu 91
Kyoto 14
    Arashiyama bamboo grove
      17

L

Lamprocapnos spectabilis
    'Alba' 275
larch 30, 32–3, 52, 53, 54, 75,
    94, 176
Levisticum officinale 173, 274
Liatris
    pycnostachya 210, 277
    spicata 206, 277
lichens 40
Ligularia 'The Rocket' 173, 274
Lilium
    auratum 168, 181, 194, 195,
      276
    'Claude Shride' 275
    × *dalhansonii* 275
    henryi 275
    medeoloides 86
    pardalinum var. *giganteum*
      224, 228, 274
Limonium platyphyllum syn. *L*
    latifolium 277
Lloyd, Christopher 70
logging industry 30, 32–3,
    47–8, 52, 53, 54, 75, 119
Lysichiton 90
    camtschatcensis 96, 99
Lysimachia
    clethroides 4, 173, 190, 276
    europaea 86

M

Magnolia 40, 75
    denudata 180, 275
    kobus 177, 277
    kobus var. *borealis* 194, 276
    obovata 72–3, 177
Maianthemum
    dilatatum 184, 185, 275
    japonica 275
Malus sieboldii 215, 224, 224,
    226, 226, 274, 276, 277
Marriot, Michael 139
Matteuccia struthiopteris 91,
    143, 275

Meadow Garden 4, 9, 9, 10, 41, 60–1, 62, 65, 68–9, 71, 75, 104, 128, 134, 146–8, 149–236, 150–2, 154–5, 166–7, 242–3, 246
  colour 164, 214, 215
  dominant species 247
  Garden Academy 246, 256
  indigenous species 169, 172, 173, 177, 180, 194, 247
  Mix A 215, 224, 224–5, 274
  Mix B 215, 222–3, 274
  Mix C 165, 208–9, 210–11, 214, 215, 218–21, 220, 274
  Mix D1 157, 160, 178, 178–9, 180, 184, 184–5, 274, 275
  Mix D2 178, 178–9, 180, 184, 184–5, 275
  Mix E1 181–2, 186–7, 275
  Mix E2 275
  Mix F 168, 194, 194–7, 212–13, 276
  Mix G1 190, 192–3, 276
  Mix G2 190, 190–3, 276
  Mix H 189, 198, 198–9, 276
  Mix I 188–91, 189, 276
  Mix J 158–9, 204–5, 215, 226, 226–7, 228, 276
  Mix K 165, 208–13, 210, 210–13, 222–3, 277
  Mix L 174–5, 206, 206–9, 277
  Mix M 174–5, 200, 204–5, 208–9, 228, 230–1, 277
  Mix N 214, 216, 216–17, 277
  naturalism 149, 153, 169, 172, 235
  paths 149, 150–1, 152, 153, 154–5, 156, 200, 252
  perennials 200–1, 277
  plant matrix 156, 157, 161, 247
  plant mix plan 156, 170–1, 172–3
  plant propagation 247, 261
  planting principles 153, 156
  seasonal planning 241–52
  seed saving 261
  staking 252
  sukashi 252
  thawing with charcoal 41, 244, 248–9
  weeding 247
  woodland glade 177, 180–1, 194, 198
  woodland wrap and planted buffer 176–7, 277

meadowsweet 169
Millennium Hill 19, 24–5, 36–9, 58, 60–1, 103
Millesgården 69, 262
Miscanthus 215
  sinensis 31, 44, 46, 148
  sinensis 'Zebrinus' 10, 215, 220, 222–3, 274
  miyamaenreiso 91
Miyamura, Yoko 266
mizubasho 96
momiji 256
mown areas 108–9

N
native forest 30, 42–3
naturalism 64, 65, 68, 69, 149, 153, 169, 172, 235
nature worship in Japan 29, 44–9, 64
Nepeta transcaucasica 'Blue Infinity' 206, 206–7, 208–9, 277
Nicotiana mutabilis 125, 126–7
nirinso 82
Noro, Kiichi 260
Norihiro, Kanekiyo 21

O
o-itadori 92–3
o-sakuraso 82
o-ubayuri 80
Obihiro 30, 58
Omori Garden 172, 215
Ono, Yoko 58
onsen 21
Orchard 60–1, 68, 120–1, 125, 132, 138, 143
Origanum laevigatum 164, 200, 202, 277
Osmundastrum cinnamomeum 87
oyama-odamaki 86

P
Pachysandra terminalis 190, 276
Paeonia
  'Buckeye Belle' 135, 156
  lactiflora 'White Wings' 275
  mlokosewitschii 274
  obovata 215, 224, 274, 275
  'Scarlet O'Hara' 274

Panicum virgatum 215
  'Heavy Metal' 174–5, 200, 202, 208–9
Paris polyphylla 83
pasture 54, 58, 68
paths and walkways 9, 22, 54, 58, 65, 78, 252
  art trail 58
  boardwalks 74, 149, 150–1, 152, 200
  riding routes 75
Patrinia scabiosifolia 214, 274
Pearson, Dan 8, 9, 9, 62, 70, 71, 94, 240, 241
  Garden Academy 246, 256
  Hillside 272–3, 273
Pennisetum alopecuroides var. viridescens 202, 202, 204–5, 230–1
Persicaria
  alpina 161, 178, 181, 188–9, 189, 194, 275, 276
  amplexicaulis 'Alba' 168, 194, 195, 196–7, 212–13, 276
  amplexicaulis 'Atrosanguinea' 162–3, 164, 165, 210, 210, 277
persimmon 140, 143
Petasites japonicus subsp. giganteus 78, 84–5, 142, 143
Peucedanum verticillare 274
Phlox paniculata 'David' 168, 181, 194, 194, 212–13, 276
Pinus
  montana 220, 277
  mugo 176–7, 214
plant laboratory 135, 138, 252, 253–5, 256, 257
Polemonium yezoense var. hidakanum 'Purple Rain' 210, 210, 277
pollution 48
Polygonatum odoratum 157, 179, 184, 185, 274, 275
Potentilla
  fruticosa 214, 277
  nepalensis 'Miss Willmott' 200, 202, 277
Primula 69
  jesoana 82
Productive Gardens 60–1, 65, 68, 75, 119–44, 120–4
  companion planting 118
  Cutting Garden 126–7, 129
  Kitchen Garden 116–18, 119, 124, 125, 128–31, 140–4, 141, 142, 143, 144, 145, 152
  Orchard 68, 120–1, 125, 132, 138, 143

Rose Garden 60–1, 68, 132, 133–8, 139, 143, 144
  stock beds 122–3
propagation 247, 261
Prunus × yedoensis 16
Pulmonaria 181
  angustifolia 'Blaues Meer' 184, 275
  'Blue Ensign' 276
  'Northern Lights' 190, 276
Pumpkin 'Rouge Vif d'Etampes' 116–17

Q
Quercus mongolica subsp. crispula 30, 40, 54, 75, 97, 177, 277

R
re-wilding 54, 55
Reynoutria japonica syn. Fallopia japonica 63, 143
Rhododendron brachytricum 277
Rodgersia 156
  'Bronze Beauty' 215, 224, 225, 274
  podophylla 182–3, 186–7, 224, 274, 275
Rosa
  damascena 132
  gallica 'Tuscany Superb' 134
  gallica var. officinalis 132
  glauca 132, 139, 160, 161, 164, 198, 200, 201, 202, 202, 224, 226, 226, 274, 276, 277
  'The Alexandra Rose' 139
  'The Lady's Blush' 135
  'The Lark Ascending' 134, 139
  macrophylla 133
  'Morning Mist' 139
  moyesii 132, 215, 224, 274
  'Munstead Wood' 279
  rubiginosa syn. R. eglanteria 139
  rugosa 277
  'Scharlachglut' 194, 245, 276
  sericea subsp. omeiensis f. pteracantha 132, 178, 179, 180, 274, 275
  spinosissima 134, 135, 139
  'winterizing' 139

Rose Garden 60–1, 68, 132, 133–8, 139, 143, 144, 244, 245
Rosendals Trädgård 69, 262
Rudbeckia
    fulgida var. *sullivantii* 'Goldsturm' 165, 214, 220, 220, 274
    laciniata 98

S
sabi 15
Saihoji temple moss garden 16, 17
sakura 16
Salix 75, 103, 150–1, 177
    alba var. *sericea* 177, 277
    purpurea 'Nancy Saunders' 194, 276
Salvia nemorosa 'Caradonna' 173, 200, 202, 202, 226, 226, 276, 277
Sambucus
    nigra 'Black Lace' 180, 274, 275
    racemosa subsp. *kamtschatica* 180
Sanguisorba 252
    albiflora 274
    'Cangshan Cranberry' 158–9, 226, 226, 228, 276
    hakusanensis 214, 216, 217, 235, 277
    officinalis 'Red Thunder' 164, 224, 225, 228, 236, 274
    tenuifolia var. *alba* 226, 226, 276
sansho 140
Sapporo 16, 29, 41
Sasa nipponica 20, 41, 52, 53, 55, 55, 59, 75, 88–9, 90, 97
Sasagawa, Shintaro 11, 70, 71, 252, 253, 260, 263, 265, 266, 267, 269
satoyama 47, 48, 49, 53, 58, 63, 65, 70, 119, 124, 263, 273
scale 53, 58, 68
seasons
    Japan's 72 seasons 232, 235, 256
    planning for 241–52
    plant laboratory 252, 253–5, 256, 257
    thawing 248–9
sedges 69
seed saving 261

Seikan Tunnel 29
Selinum wallichianum 275
shakkei 65, 103–4, 107, 149, 176–7
Shimizu Forestry Association 21, 94
Shintani, Midori 8, 9, 9, 11, 41, 45, 68–70, 71, 78, 90, 95, 96, 104, 141, 172–3, 233, 240, 241, 252, 259, 260, 263, 265, 266, 267
    'Finding your own wild' 232–6
    'From earth to table' 140–4
    Garden Academy 246, 256
    'The gardenership' 264–9
    'Hands for the Forest' 94–8
    'Nature worship in Japan' 44–8
    plant laboratory 252, 253–5, 256, 257
    training 69, 262, 269
Shinto *see* nature worship in Japan
shirakanba 20
shiraneaoi 82
shun 140, 143
skunk cabbage 40, 78
snow 34, 35, 40–1, 112–13, 114, 115, 241
    thawing with charcoal 41, 244, 248–9
traditional Japanese buildings 258–9
snowmelt 22, 35, 40, 40, 41, 47, 153
soil 35
Solidago gigantea 98
Sorbaria sorbifolia 177, 277
Sorbus commixta 177, 277
Sparkes, Joshua 267
Stachys byzantina 206, 206–7, 277
stepping stones 23, 64
Stewartia
    japonica 161
    pseudocamellia 178, 180, 185, 188, 190, 192–3, 275, 276
Stipa barbata 277
stock beds 122–3
stones 64, 75, 200
    Circle of Kamui 60-1, 103, 104
    erratics 20, 21, 35
student gardeners 70, 260, 263, 266–7

Succisa pratensis 204–5
sukashi 252
sustainability 21, 22, 53, 54, 75
susuki 148
Symphyotrichum turbinellum 179, 181, 184, 188, 189, 190, 275, 276
Symplocarpus foetidus 83
syuroso 87

T
tachi-giboshi 87
Takada, Mizuho 267
Takano, Fumiaki/Takano Landscape Planning 8, 16, 20, 21–2, 54, 62, 94, 97, 107
Tanizaki, Junichiro
    In Praise of Shadows 15
Tashiro Forest 59
tea ceremony 69, 262, 269
Tellima grandiflora 275
Thalictrum 69, 169
    aquilegiifolium 194, 276
    baicalense 87
    delavayi 210, 277
    delavayi 'Album' 275
    'Elin' 214, 220, 220, 274
    flavum subsp. *glaucum* 214, 220, 274
    minus var. *hypoleucum* 84–5
    'Splendide' 210, 212–13, 275, 277
Thermopsis lupinoides 172–3, 274
Tiarella 'Sugar and Spice' 190, 276
Tokachi 16, 41
Tokachi Mainichi Newspaper Company 21
Tokachi Millennium Forest 48
    annual planning 241–52
    design 53–70
    plan 60–1
    shakkei 65, 103–4, 107, 149
    site 21–2, 53–4, 55, 65, 94, 103, 106
Tokachi Shimizu 94
tomoeso 87
Tradescantia (Andersoniana Group) 'Innocence' 188–9, 189, 276
Tricyrtis 'Tojen' 184, 275
Trifolium rubens 226, 226, 276
Trillium 69, 172
    camschatcense 97, 182–3, 275
    tschonoskii 91

Trollius × *cultorum* 'Yellow Queen' 184, 184–5, 275
Tsugaru Strait 29
tsumatoriso 86

U
urbanization 22, 48

V
Valeriana officinalis 214, 216, 216, 233, 277
Veratrum
    album subsp. *oxysepalum* 63, 83, 86, 91
    maackii 87, 275
    nigrum 275
Verbascum 'Christo's Yellow Lightning' 274
Vernonia
    arkansana 'Mammuth' 158–9, 204–5, 226, 226, 228, 276
    fasciculata 158–9, 226, 228, 229, 276
Veronicastrum
    sibiricum 198, 198, 200, 226, 226, 276
    sibiricum subsp. *yezoense* 158–9, 226, 226, 228, 276
volcanic terrain 22

W
wabi 15
Wachter, Michael 267
watercourses 34, 35
wildlife 41, 54

Y
yamabukishoma 76–7, 81, 87
yamadori-zenmai 87
yomogi 140

Z
Zanthoxylum piperitum 140
zazenso 83
Zen gardens 63
Zenge, Mitsuko 266

ACKNOWLEDGEMENTS

This book is dedicated to Mitsushige Hayashi, the visionary and the enabler. Without your oversight and the support of your sons, none of this would be possible.

The Millennium Forest is, by definition, a team effort. The place inspires devotion and many have fallen under its spell and each, in their own way, have helped to provide momentum. Staff, students and visitors, this place is made live through your participation.

Thank you, Takano, for introducing me to the project two decades ago, for giving me room to work at scale and, with the support of your office, to make things happen on the ground. You saw that this place is as much about the people as it is the preservation of the land.

Midori, you are the reason the garden breathes easy and I do too in the knowledge that it is in such wise hands. You are a good friend and collaborator. Thank you for your careful words within these pages and for your input and oversight throughout.

Shintaro, I thank you for your well-trained eye, your understanding in the garden and steadfast support to Midori. Together the two of you make at least the power of three.

Kiichi Noro, we are honoured to have you as the in-house photographer of the Millennium Forest and Shogo Oizumi, we thank you also for your earlier work. We could easily have made a photographic book that simply indulged the 72 seasons and all their nuance. The material is there.

Fergus Garrett, a warm thank you for your generosity in welcoming first the idea, and then the realisation of the Dixter gardeners exchange. I know that you have made Midori's team as welcome there as she has your students at the forest. This collaboration has been sustaining and enriched through sharing the magic and lessons of this place with a generation of young gardeners.

Huw, a special thank you for your ability to distil the essence. Your commitment to the book from the very outset has been unswerving and your eye and attention to detail are evident on every page. It is continually rewarding to partner in a vision of such shared values.

To Anna Mumford at Filbert Press, sincere thanks for your openness and constancy in making this publication happen. Your enthusiastic engagement with the project from day one has been validating. The acuity of your vision in understanding both the big picture and the detail has brought the value of the Millennium Forest into focus for us all.

Thank you, Diana Vowles, for your light and intelligent copy editing, and to publicist Emma O'Bryen, for ensuring that the message of the forest will be read as widely as possible. Dr. Jamie Compton, heartfelt thanks for untying a number of taxonomical knots and getting us on the straight and narrow.

Thank you, Julie Weiss, for being a font of enthusiasm. For making it a mission to work at the Millennium Forest so that you could understand how best to design this book. You have made the perfect partner to Huw and it has been exciting to see your combined energies in creating a book that beautifully conveys the magic of the place.

And lastly, a forever thank you to the forest. This magical piece of ground has drawn us in and then onward. You ask us to look and we find ourselves answered.

ABOUT THE AUTHORS

Follow Dan's story:
@coyotewillow
@danpearsonstudio
@digdelve
danpearsonstudio.com
digdelve.com

Follow Midori's story :
@lillajapan
tmf-garden.jp

Visit the Forest:
tmf.jp

Tokachi Millennium Forest
Minami 10sen Haobi
Shimizu-cho
Hokkaido
089-0356
Japan
Tel: 0156-63-3000
Fax: 0156-63-3031

Dan Pearson trained at the RHS Gardens, Wisley and at the Royal Botanic Gardens, Kew. Two years spent working at the botanic gardens of Jerusalem and Edinburgh increased his innate understanding of plant ecology which along with an appreciation for natural landscapes inspires his garden design today. His international work for public and private clients is widely celebrated and he has received numerous accolades including Honorary Fellow of the Royal Institute of British Architects, Royal Designer for Industry in 2012, and Society of Garden Designers awards. He has designed five award-winning Chelsea Flower Show gardens including Best in Show in 2015, writes a weekly gardening journal DIGDELVE and lectures widely.

Midori Shintani trained in horticulture and landscape architecture at Minami Kyushu University, Japan. In 2002 she moved to Sweden and trained to become a gardener at Millesgården and Rosendals Trädgård. In 2004 she moved back to Japan and worked at a garden design company and perennial nursery gaining experience in both traditional and modern styles. Since 2008 she has been the head gardener of Tokachi Millennium Forest, merging 'new Japanese horticulture' into wild nature. Midori writes and lectures widely.

PHOTO ACKNOWLEDGEMENTS

Kiichi Noro 2, 6-7, 10, 12-13, 18-19, 23, 24-25, 26-27, 31, 32-33, 34, 36-37, 38-39, 40, 42-43, 45, 46, 49, 50-51, 52, 56-57, 66-67, 71, 72-73, 74, 76-77, 79, 80, 81, 82, 83, 86-87, 91, 92-93, 99, 102, 108-109, 110, 111, 112-113, 115 (bottom), 118, 120-121, 122-123, 126-127, 128 (2 & 3), 129, 130-131, 133, 134 (1, 3 & 4), 135, 136-137, 138, 141, 146-147, 148, 150-151, 152 (4), 154-155, 157, 158-159, 160, 162-163, 165, 166-167, 174-175, 178, 179 (3 & 5), 182-183, 184 (1), 185 (2 & 3), 186-187, 188, 189, 190, 192-193, 194 (2), 195, 196-197, 199 (2, 3 & 4), 202, 203, 204-205, 206, 207, 208-209, 210 (1 & 3), 212-213, 216, 217 (3), 218-219, 220, 222-223, 224, 225, 226, 227, 229, 230-231, 234, 237, 238-239, 240, 242-243, 246, 248-249 (main), 250, 251, 252, 253, 254-255, 257, 258, 259, 265, 266 (1, 3 & 4), 267, 268 (top), 270-271, 279, 284-285

Shogo Oizumi 4, 62 (bottom), 84-85, 88-89, 95, 96, 100-101, 115 (top), 116-117, 124, 128 (1), 134 (2), 168, 179 (4), 185 (4), 191, 194 (1), 198 (1), 210 (2), 211, 217 (2), 221, 233, 245, 248 (left) 261, 262, 266 (2 & 5)

Dan Pearson 14, 17, 20, 55 (top), 106, 287

Dan Pearson Studio 62 (top left and top right), 105, 152 (1,2 & 3)

Tokachi Millennium Forest 55 (bottom), 268 (bottom)

Midori Shintani 142, 145

Huw Morgan 9, 273

Cover Photo: The Meadow Garden in autumn. The planting connects seamlessly to the borrowed view of the landscape beyond. (Photo by Kiichi Noro)

First published in 2020 by Filbert Press

filbertpress.com

Text © 2020 Dan Pearson and Midori Shintani

Editorial and Creative Director, Huw Morgan

Design by Julie Weiss

Illustrations by Duhita McNally

A catalogue record for this book is available from the British Library

ISBN: 978-1-9997345-4-1

10 9 8 7 6 5 4 3 2 1   20 21 22 23 24 25 26 27 28 29

Printed by Printer Trento S.r.l., Italy

MIX
Paper from responsible sources
FSC® C015829
www.fsc.org

This product is made of FSC® - certified paper and cloth